Contents

T0295840

First published 2021
by Routledge
2 Park Square, Milton Park, Abingdon, Oxon OX14 4RN

and by Routledge
52 Vanderbilt Avenue, New York, NY 10017

Routledge is an imprint of the Taylor & Francis Group, an informa business

© 2021 Nina Seppala

British Library Cataloguing in Publication Data
A catalogue record for this book is available from the British Library

Library of Congress Cataloging-in-Publication Data
Names: Seppälä, Nina, author.
Title: Absolute essentials of business behavioural ethics / Nina Seppala.
Description: First Edition. | New York : Routledge, 2020. | Series:
Absolute essentials of business and economics | Includes bibliographical references and index. | Identifiers: LCCN 2020018457 (print) | LCCN 2020018458 (ebook) | ISBN
9780367275402 (hardback) | ISBN 9780429296529 (ebook)
Subjects: LCSH: Business ethics. | Social responsibility of business. |
Organizational behavior.
Classification: LCC HF5387 .S447 2020 (print) | LCC HF5387 (ebook) | DDC
174/.4–dc23
LC record available at https://lccn.loc.gov/2020018457
LC ebook record available at https://lccn.loc.gov/2020018458

ISBN: 978-0-367-27540-2 (hbk)
ISBN: 978-0-429-29652-9 (ebk)

Typeset in Times New Roman
by Taylor & Francis Books

Printed in the United Kingdom
by Henry Ling Limited

Part I
Rise in behavioural ethics research

1 Introduction

Experimental approaches to the study of ethics

Learning outcomes

- Provide an overview of the factors that led to the development of behavioural ethics as a field of research.
- Explain the concept of bounded ethicality.

It is not difficult to think about a recent event that involves behaviour that most people would find unethical. The following events provide examples of unethical behaviour involving corporations, private individuals, and charitable organisations.

- Mortgage providers contributed to the financial crisis of 2007 by approving mortgage applications that did not meet the requirements set by government-sponsored bodies. Mortgages were passed to meet targets that were tied to individual bonuses and other rewards. Even after the financial crisis, this practice continued with several whistleblowers being silenced. When Sherry Hunt, a whistleblower working for Citibank, shared information about the practice with a government agency, it was found that only 70% of the mortgage applications approved by the bank satisfied the requirements against 95% reported by the bank.
- The fire of Grenfell Tower in London led to the death of over a hundred people. The fire has been described as one of the most horrible disasters in the history of modern London. There were however individuals who sought to benefit from the private donations and public support provided to the victims of the fire. In one case, a woman falsely claimed that her husband had died in the fire in order to live in a Hilton hotel and receive other benefits and support worth £19k.
- Peacekeepers and charity workers have been found to be involved in the abuse of children and other vulnerable groups in areas of

conflict and natural disaster. In 2018, it became public knowledge that Oxfam employees had abused their power by hiring prostitutes in Haiti. Some of the prostitutes may have been under-age and highly vulnerable in the conditions following the earthquake in the country. Oxfam dismissed four staff members, but did not warn other organisations about the involvement of its former staff in prostitution.

There has been a surge of studies in behavioural ethics to understand why people behave in such unethical ways. The emergence of research in behavioural ethics has reflected developments in research technologies that have enabled the research community to draw new insights about the drivers of ethical and unethical behaviour. While behavioural ethics is a relatively new area of research, there are earlier studies in experimental psychology that have implications for the study of ethics. For example, Stanley Milgram studied obedience to authority in the 1960s in a series of experiments where participants were asked to administer electric shocks to another person. Milgram's studies demonstrated that individuals rarely question authority even when they are asked to perform actions that are harmful for other people. Similarly, Philip Zimbardo ran an experiment about prison conditions in the 1970s at Stanford University. The experiment suggested that people adjust their behaviour to social norms and can behave in ways that they would not normally find acceptable. These studies are discussed in more detail in Chapter 2 as examples of early studies in behavioural ethics.

The new studies in behavioural ethics have tailed the development of brain imaging technology that has enabled neuroscientists to study the areas of the brain activated by ethical issues (e.g. Cushman et al., 2011). One of the findings has been that ethical issues activate both cognitive and emotional areas of the brain. More specifically, moral dilemmas pertaining to physical harm or commonly accepted norms activate brain areas responsible for the processing of emotions and, without the activation of emotions, moral judgements, and ethical behaviour relating to these issues changes (Koenigs et al., 2007). Another finding has been that people react to ethical dilemmas quickly based on their moral intuition without using deliberate decision-making (Haidt, 2001). Accordingly, moral judgements result from sudden feelings of approval or disapproval in our consciousness. Reasoning is predominantly employed to rationalise and explain the ethical choices that have been made on the basis of instinctive intuitions or what Bauman (1993) referred to as the moral impulse. Moral reasoning is also used to consider new situations and cases where intuition is not clear (Haidt, 2001).

As a result, ethical decision-making and behaviour seem to take place intuitively based on learnt responses rather than through a rational consideration of different alternatives (Haidt, 2001). Haidt (2001) referred to the new findings about ethical behaviour as the emotional turn to highlight the importance of emotions in triggering ethical behaviour.

The intuitive nature of ethical decision-making is connected to the concept of bounded ethicality which refers to the unconscious nature of many ethical decisions (Bazerman and Tenbrunsel, 2011). Bounded ethicality means that people engage in unethical behaviour against their own values and intentions without realising that it is happening. The new experimental studies have been influenced by the bounded nature of ethical behaviour with researchers being interested in discovering hidden or unconscious factors that influence ethical behaviour.

It has been challenging to agree on a definition of ethics that would underpin experimental studies about ethical behaviour. In moral philosophy, theories of ethics explore the principles of right and wrong in reference to arguments about human nature. Many well-known philosophers have proposed universal principles that apply to all human beings on the basis of arguments about human dignity and what it means to lead a meaningful life. Other, more post-modernist thinkers have argued that universal principles are not achievable and it is only possible to conceive ethical standards for particular situations. In the context of behavioural ethics, ethical behaviour has been defined as the actions that do not harm others and are neither 'illegal or morally unacceptable to the larger community' (Jones, 1991). This definition ties ethics to commonly accepted standards of behaviour which may be incorporated in the law. However, the definition has been criticised because there are historical and current examples of shared standards that are not ethical, including slavery and child labour. Similarly, while laws often reflect ethical principles, laws can also encompass standards that would be difficult to defend on ethical grounds.

The difficulties in finding a definition of ethics that would provide a basis for behavioural studies has led many researchers to relate their work to the concept of dishonesty rather than ethics. In studies about dishonesty, ethical behaviour is framed as the opportunity to lie, steal, and perform other acts that most people would view as unethical in most circumstances. There is however a question about the applicability of the findings of these studies to other ethical decisions and behaviours. For example, people may be driven by self-interest to lie in order to accrue financial resources, but they would not cause physical harm to other people in order to benefit financially. It is therefore important to be cautious about the findings of experimental studies and how relevant they are for different types of ethical issues and decisions.

Until recently, the study of ethics has been strongly influenced by philosophical theories of the right and wrong. For example, insights from philosophy have been used to study whether people apply a utilitarian or a more rights-based approach to making decisions about ethics. The focus has been on understanding the different perspectives and arguments that can be made about a particular situation and recommending how individuals and organisations should behave on the basis of philosophical notions. In parallel, ethics has been studied as an area of developmental psychology to understand how individuals develop values and cognitive approaches for thinking through situations that involve moral choices (Kohlberg, 1984). In contrast to these more philosophical and developmental approaches, behavioural ethics emerged in the 2000s with a focus on studying how people really behave in situations involving moral choices, not how they should behave.

In parallel to the emergence of an increasing number of experimental studies about ethics in psychology, there has been a similar growth in the number of ethics studies in the field of behavioural economics. This growth has been fuelled by research findings suggesting that people do not always behave rationally to advance their self-interest. For example, in studies about tax evasion and corruption, researchers have found that while people are sensitive to sanctions and other incentives, they do not cheat as much as they would be expected to cheat based on the assumption that their behaviour is motivated by the goal of maximising their income and avoiding penalties (Irlenbusch and Villeval, 2015). As a result, research in behavioural economics has grown to understand the factors that explain the dynamics underpinning the honesty and dishonesty of economics actors. Studies in behavioural economics share a number of variables, measures, and experimental designs with studies in psychology, but there are also additional concepts studied in economics, including information asymmetry, externalities, and market institutions.

The focus in behavioural ethics research has been on the psychological processes and social or organisational factors that explain how people behave. One area of research has been the individual factors and psychological dynamics that influence ethical decision-making and behaviour. For example, a new concept in this area is the idea of a moral equilibrium which refers to the mental balance that people seem to unconsciously hold about their behaviour. Such individual influences on ethical behaviour are discussed in Part II of the book. Another set of experiments has focussed on the study of social and environmental factors that influence ethical behaviour. In this area of study, it has been found that people's behaviour is affected by the norms of the community they belong to. Social and other situational factors are reviewed in Part II of the book.

In sum, responses to ethical dilemmas reflect a combination of factors that come together about the decision-maker's individual characteristics, the wider situation including social norms, and the nature of the ethical issue itself. Behavioural ethics has been influenced by studies in neuroscience which suggest that ethical decision-making and behaviour can take place quickly and unconsciously. Studies in behavioural ethics often explore honesty and dishonesty because the research community has not agreed on a definition of ethics or a categorisation of ethical issues that would provide a framework for the study of behavioural ethics. Behavioural ethics research has taken place in both psychology and economics with similar research designs, variables, and measures. In psychology, research in behavioural ethics can be categorised into individual and situational factors, while research in economics also involves more market and societal level concepts such as externalities and market institutions.

Key readings

Haidt, J. 2008. Morality. *Perspectives on Psychological Science* 3 (1), 65–72.
Jonathan Haidt developed the social intuitionist model of moral judgement. In this article, he provides a review of how moral psychology has developed as a field from the work of Emile Durkheim to today's affective and evolutionary approaches to morality.

Mock assessment questions

- What developments led to the emergence of behavioural ethics as a field of research?
- How would you define ethics? What are the limitations of this definition?
- What is meant by the notion of bounded ethicality and how does it relate to the emotional turn in the study of ethics?

Class exercise

Ask students to spend three minutes online, identifying one recent event involving unethical behaviour. Students should be able to summarise the event, what is (un)ethical about it, and the consequences of the event for individuals and other affected parties. Randomly ask five students to share the details of the event they identified.

2 Historical experiments in the study of ethics

Learning outcomes

- Explain the implications of the Milgram studies and the Stanford Prison Experiment for the study of ethics.
- Be able to discuss the limitations of the Milgram studies and the Stanford Prison Experiment.

The Milgram studies on obedience to authority and the Stanford Prison Experiment are some of the best-known studies in the history of social psychology. They are reviewed in this chapter to explore their implications for the study of ethical behaviour. Even though both studies were framed as studies about other phenomena, they both relate to behaviour that people would generally find unacceptable. Indeed, research participants themselves were surprised about their behaviour during the experiments.

Milgram obedience to authority experiments

Some of the earliest experimental studies shedding light on ethical behaviour were conducted by Stanley Milgram at Yale University in the 1960s. Milgram's studies about obedience to authority showed that individuals are reluctant to disobey authority, even when they are asked to carry out questionable acts. Milgram (1965) later summarised the results of his studies by concluding that 'in certain circumstances it is not so much the kind of person a man is, as the kind of situation in which he is placed, that determines how he will act'.

Milgram started his research in the aftermath of the trial of Adolf Eichmann who had worked in the Nazi regime during the Second World War supervising deportations to extermination camps. Eichmann's defence argued that he was following the orders of higher authorities without agreeing to the goals of the regime. The trial was witnessed by Hannah Arendt (1964) who observed that Eichmann's actions were predominantly motivated by professional ambition rather than ideology. Arendt saw Eichmann as a mundane and average person who spoke in clichés and did not seem to think for himself. It is in this context that Milgram was interested in understanding the role of authority and obedience in 'evil' acts such as the organised genocide that took place during the Second World War. Milgram (1963) started the article in which he described his experiments by saying:

> Gas chambers were built, death camps were guarded, daily quotas of corpses were produced with the same efficiency as the manufacture of appliances. These inhumane policies may have originated in the mind of a single person, but they could only be carried out on a massive scale if a very large number of persons obeyed orders.

Milgram (1965) recruited a total of 40 male participants for his first study about obedience through newspapers adverts. The participants were told that the study was about the effect of punishment on learning. The experimental set-up involved three people: an experimenter, a teacher, and a learner. Upon arrival, the participants were instructed to take a slip of paper from a hat to determine whether they would play the role of a teacher or a learner. In reality, the draw was rigged and each participant became a teacher who was instructed to teach pairs of words to a learner. A 47-year-old accountant played the role of the learner, while the role of the experimenter was played by a high-school biology teacher wearing a laboratory coat.

In the experiment, the learner was seated into a chair and connected to an electrode in a separate room. The participants read a series of words to the learner through an intercom system and the learner communicated his answers through switches that lit an answer box placed in the front of the participant. The participants were instructed to administer electric shocks to the learner if the learner made mistakes. They were shown to use a mock generator with voltage levels ranging from 15 to 450 to administer the shocks. The volts were described on the generator as varying from 'slight shock' to 'danger: severe shock'. The participants were told that 'although the shocks can be extremely painful, they cause no permanent tissue damage'. Their instruction was to administer a shock each time the learner gave an incorrect answer and to increase the voltage every time they administered a new shock. When the shocks reached 300 volts, the learner pounded on the wall of the room where he was located. This pounding was repeated at 315 volts after which the learner made no sound or gave no answers. The experimenter encouraged the participants to continue giving electric shocks, using a set of pre-designed sentences to respond to any queries from the participants. If a participant refused to apply a shock after four such sentences were used, the experiment ended.

Out of 40 participants, 65% of the participants administered the highest level of electric shocks. A smaller proportion of 35% of the participants refused to administer the shocks, although they only started to do so at 300 volts when the learner pounded the wall of his room. The participants often expressed reluctance to administer the shocks and showed signs of stress, but they obeyed the orders of the experimenter. Many of the participants sweated, bit their lips, and verbally objected to the administration of shocks, but continued to follow instructions. Milgram (1963) found this reaction extraordinary: 'One might suppose that a subject would simply break off or continue as his conscience dictated. Yet, this is very far from what happened. There were striking reactions of tension and emotional strain'.

After the first experiment, Milgram continued to run experiments about obedience, involving almost a thousand participants in the studies. He varied conditions in the experiments to have a better understanding of when people would disobey an authority. For example, after observing that participants turned their eyes away from the learner when they administered electric shocks, Milgram explored whether obedience diminished when the learner became more salient to the participant. He changed the location of the learner in four different ways. The first condition was identical to the original experiment. In the second condition, the voice feedback condition, the learner's voice and complaints could be heard from another room. In the third condition the learner was placed in the same room with the participant so that voice and visual signals were directly observable. In the final and fourth condition, the participant had to physically move the learner's hand to a shock plate when a level of 150 volts was reached because the learner refused to do this himself. The results showed that 34% of the participants disobeyed the experimenter when the learner was in another room, 37.5% in the voice feedback condition, 60% when the learner was in the same room, and 70% when physical contact was involved. The proximity of the victim therefore increased disobedience and is an important way of countering the power of authority.

Milgram (1965) also varied the physical closeness of the authority in another series of studies. In the first condition the experimenter sat in the same room with the participants, in the second condition the experimenter saw the participant first in person and then left to deliver the instructions over the phone, and in the third condition the instructions were given through a tape recording. Obedience decreased across the three conditions. The number of participants who disobeyed the experimenter was three times higher in the second condition where instructions were given over the phone than in the first condition where the experimenter remained in the room. Moreover, when the experimenter was not present, the participants lied about the severance of the shocks they administered and gave the learners lower level shocks from the ones instructed. These findings suggest that the effect of authority diminishes when the authority is not physically present.

Milgram's experiments made an important contribution by showing that environmental conditions have an important influence on individual behaviour. The findings demonstrate that individuals are reluctant to question authority and even when they do so, they may keep complying with unethical norms and practices. Furthermore, some of the effect of authority and obedience can be countered by closeness to the victim and distance from authority. Milgram also noted that the effect of the experimenter's position is stronger on the behaviour of the participant than the effect of the learner-victim. In the context of organisations, the findings suggest that the role of managers is important in enabling or reducing ethical behaviour.

The Stanford Prison Experiment

The Stanford Prison Experiment (1971) was designed to investigate the effects of a simulated prison environment on the behaviour of guards and prisoners, but some of the effects also shed light on ethical behaviour and how it evolves in a particular organisational context. The experiment was led by Dr Philip Zimbardo from Stanford University who later on wrote a book, *The Lucifer Effect* (2007), about the deterioration of ethical behaviour through the dehumanisation of others, uncritical conformity to group norms, and other processes. The experiment shows how individual behaviour is influenced by the organisational role and related expectations a person has, but also the different ways in which individuals respond to organisational structures and policies.

Dr Zimbardo and his team recruited volunteers for the study through an advert in a local newspaper in the Palo Alto area of California. More than 70 volunteers responded to the advert that called for male students 'to participate in psychological study of prison life'. The research team selected 24 students for the study who were described as healthy, intelligent, and middle-class. The volunteers signed a contract that informed them about conditions during the study including a minimally adequate diet and potential for some intimidation. The volunteers were then divided into guards and prisoners on a flip of a coin. The experiment started with nine guards and nine prisoners. The remaining volunteers were requested to be on call in case any of the guards or prisoners needed to be replaced.

The simulated prison environment was constructed in the cellar of the psychology department at Stanford. The research team boarded up a corridor and created a prison-like atmosphere by replacing doors with steel bars and cell numbers. A camera was installed to film events in the corridor and an intercom system was used to listen to discussions among guards and prisoners. Altogether three cells were created with each of the cells containing three beds. A small closet across from the cells was used as a solitary confinement unit. The guards had a set of rooms in an adjacent corridor for breaks and changing facilities. The guards worked in shifts of eight hours and only spent their working shift in the prison environment.

The volunteers who became prisoners were picked up from their home in a police car. They were delivered to the prison blindfolded. Upon arrival, each prisoner was stripped naked, searched, and sprayed for any germs. They were then issued a uniform which had their prison number on the front and in the back. They were given no undergarments and instructed to use hair protection to make them feel emasculated and awkward. The prisoners were referred to by their number rather than their name throughout the experiment. A heavy chain and a lock were placed on their right ankle to be worn day and night. The guards wore khaki uniforms, a whistle, a police stick, and sunglasses that prevented eye contact. Their task was to maintain 'a reasonable degree of order' among the prisoners, although physical aggression was distinctly prohibited.

No specific incidents took place during the first day of the experiment. Because of this, the research team was surprised when there was a rebellion on the second morning of the experiment. The prisoners barricaded themselves inside the cells by blocking the doors with their beds. In response, the guards used a fire extinguisher to force the prisoners away from the doors and broke in to each cell. They then stripped the prisoners of clothing and put the perceived leaders into solitary confinement. They also created a privilege cell and placed the best behaved prisoners into this cell. Privileged prisoners were given back their beds and prison clothes. They were also allowed to eat food when other prisoners were not. After a while, the guards mixed the prisoners, creating suspicion that the prisoners from the privileged cell now acted as informants. The guards also started treating toilet visits and many other normal activities as a privilege.

After less than 36 hours, one prisoner started to show signs of emotional distress through uncontrollable crying and anger. He was given an offer to become an informant in exchange for no harassment from the guards. He however continued to show symptoms of distress and was released later on during the day. Another prisoner wanted to see a doctor. Instead, he was asked to rest in an adjacent room while a doctor was fetched. Before this happened, one of the guards made other prisoners shout that the prisoner feeling ill was a bad prisoner. The unwell prisoner started to sob and refused to leave the prison until Zimbardo reminded him about the experiment and his role as a volunteer, not a real prisoner. A total of five prisoners were released before the experiment ended on the sixth day because of crying, rage, and anxiety.

The experiment was ended after the research team became aware that the guards had escalated their abuse when they thought they were not being observed by the research team. For example, greater harassment took place on the way to the toilet when the guards believed they were not being filmed or recorded. The ethicality of the experiment was also questioned by a researcher, Dr Zimbardo's girlfriend who had been brought in to interview the participants. She was horrified by the behaviour she saw in the simulated environment and insisted that the experiment was stopped. The experiment had lasted for six days instead of the two weeks it had been planned for.

The researchers were surprised to see how quickly 'a sample of normal, healthy American college students fractionate into a group of prison guards who seemed to derive pleasure from insulting, threatening, humiliating and dehumanising their peers' (Zimbardo, 2007, p. 89). The guards initially responded aggressively to the rebellion of the prisoners in the beginning of the experiment. The behaviour of the guards escalated over time and continued even when the prisoners showed signs of emotional distress and submission. The most aggressive guards emerged as leaders who gave commands and invented punishments. Their behaviour was not contradicted by other guards in an atmosphere where not to be tough was a sign of weakness. When interviewed after the experiment, guards explained their behaviour by saying that they were playing the role of guards, which shows how role expectations can influence behaviour and create patterns of behaviour that would not be acceptable in another environment.

The research team identified three types of guards. First, there were 'tough but fair' guards (p. 81) who followed rules to maintain order.

Second, there were passive guards who rarely applied any coercive measures on the prisoners and occasionally carried out little favours for the prisoners. Finally, there were hostile guards who sought to humiliate the prisoners and were inventive in doing so. The most hostile guard known as 'John Wayne' has been particularly clear in his interviews since the experiment took place that he was playing a role and sought to instigate a reaction among the prisoners so that the researchers would have material for their study. Also, there was variation in the behaviour of different groups of guards. The evening shift was the harshest in terms of the number of commands made by the guards (9.30 versus 4.04 commands) and the insults used towards prisoners (5.17 versus 2.29 insults) over periods of 2.5 hours. The night shift from 10pm to 6am was the least abusive one for the prisoners except for an early morning count of prisoners.

Despite the individual differences in the extent and type of aggression used by guards, the research team was not able to establish a link between guard behaviour and personality traits. Most of the findings about personality were connected to the behaviour and endurance of the prisoners. As a result, the researchers concluded that personality traits and attitudes account for only a small degree of variation in individual behaviour. Instead, it is situational forces, the qualities of the prison environment that have a significant influence on how individuals behave. Zimbardo's team was therefore successful in demonstrating their original aim that it is not the characteristics of correctional staff or inmates that create violence and degrading conditions in prisons. The findings of the experiment are also interesting for understanding the importance of organisational roles and expectations for explaining ethical behaviour and have contributed to the idea of 'bounded ethicality'.

The Stanford Prison Experiment has been criticised for causing distress to the participants and for projecting of researcher expectations on the participants. In addition to the ethical issues related to creating conditions where the participants experienced emotional and physical distress, critics have argued that Zimbardo became involved in the experiment and assumed a role of a participant rather than a detached researcher (Trevino, 1992). He has been criticised for leading the guards and taking measures to evoke a sense of humiliation among the prisoners. For example, in the orientation meeting with the guards, he said: 'We can create boredom. We can create a sense of frustration. We can create fear in them, to some degree … We have total power over the situation. They have none' (Blum, 2018). Furthermore, it has been revealed later that one of the research assistants had the responsibility to provoke 'tough guard' behaviour (Blum, 2018). The research assistant directed individual guards on multiple occasions to become tougher over the course of the experiment. As a result, the behaviour of the guards did not emerge organically as originally suggested by Zimbardo.

The research team has also been criticised for the interpretation of the motives and behaviour of the volunteers. For example, one prisoner has later revealed that he pretended emotional distress in order to leave the experiment once he realised he couldn't prepare for his examinations during the experiment (Blum, 2018). Critics have also argued that Zimbardo was an authority figure for the guards who identified with him and his goals for the experiment (Haslam and Reicher, 2012). Because of this, Zimbardo's original argument that the guards developed the rules for the simulated prison environment with little instruction from the researchers has been discredited. Finally, the experiment was designed to explore how relatively well-educated and emotionally stable individuals behave in exceptional conditions. The findings may therefore not apply beyond this population and if a more mixed, heterogeneous sample had been used, the results might have been different.

Overall, the Stanford Prison Experiment shows that environmental factors have an important effect on ethical behaviour, but personal characteristics also play a role. It is the balance between the environment and the person that explains how an individual reacts to an ethical dilemma. The small and homogenous sample did not allow the researchers to explore the interaction between personality and behaviour and the experiment therefore leaves open the question about the effect of personal characteristics on ethical behaviour and the more detailed processes through which ethical or unethical behaviour evolves. One of the most striking findings of the Stanford Prison Experiment was that no guard ever questioned the humiliating and abusive behaviour of other guards even when the prisoners demonstrated stress and anxiety. This aspect of group cohesion and solidarity has received little attention in later research exploring ethical behaviour, but it has been elaborated upon in more political and philosophical writings about totalitarianism and unethical behaviour.

Key readings

Haslam, S. A., and Reicher, S. D. 2012. Contesting the 'nature' of conformity: What Milgram and Zimbardo's studies really show. *PLOS Biology* 10 (11), e1001426.

In this article, two researchers provide a critical evaluation of the Milgram studies and the Stanford Prison Experiment. Zimbardo has been critical about the arguments made in the article and has provided a public reply to the criticism presented in the article.

Milgram, S. 1965. Some conditions of obedience and disobedience to authority. *Human Relations* 18, 57–76.

This is an original article by Milgram about his studies in obedience and authority. The experimental design is explained in detail and a brief review of experiments following the original study is provided.

Mock assessment questions

- What are the implications of the findings of the Milgram Studies and the Stanford Prison Experiment for the study of ethics?
- What are the main criticisms presented about the Stanford Prison Experiment? Do these criticisms mean that the findings are invalid?

Class exercise

Show students the following interview of one of the guards in the Stanford Prison Experiment: https://www.youtube.com/watch?v=fQnOkmvigi0 (also available at https://www.prisonexp.org/). Ask students why the guard only questioned his behaviour after the experiment had taken place, not during the experiment.

3 Measuring ethics in experiments

Learning outcomes

- Discuss internal and external validity of experimental designs.
- Describe experiments that have been used to measure dishonesty and unethical behaviour.

Studying ethical or unethical behaviour is difficult because unethical behaviour is typically hidden. People are likely to conceal their unethical behaviour and cannot be expected to voluntarily disclose information about their dishonest behaviour. Studying ethics is also difficult because research participants may be affected by social desirability bias and alter their behaviour in alignment with study objectives or what they believe the ideal behaviour is (Trevino, 1992). Until the emergence of behavioural ethics research, surveys were used to study ethical behaviour. Up to 80% of research in behavioural ethics was based in surveys until the 1990s (Randall and Gibson, 1990). Only 6% of studies published in peer reviewed journals consisted of experimental research (Ibid.). The disadvantage of surveys is that they rely on self-reported attitudes and behaviour, which may not correspond to actual behaviour. When survey results have been compared to real unethical behaviour in the form of tax evasion, there has been a positive correlation, but the correlation has been a weak one (Hessing et al., 1988). The emerging research in behavioural ethics helps to address some of the concerns over survey based self-reports, but experimental designs come with their own challenges relating to internal and external validity.

Experimental research consists of the design of activities through which one or more independent variables can be manipulated and observing changes in the dependent variable. The two principal forms of experimental research are laboratory research and field research. Laboratory research is carried out in artificial settings where the researcher has a high degree of control over the variables being measured, which enhances internal validity defined as the relationship between the observed variables. Laboratory research also has the benefit of a random allocation of participants to the experimental and control conditions, which decreases the possibility that other, confounding variables influence changes in the dependent variable. In contrast, field research is carried out in natural settings where the researcher observes the independent and dependent variables in real situations. Field research has the advantage of a real setting and this is why it is often seen to have a high degree of external validity meaning that the findings apply to real situations that are more complex than laboratory settings. The challenge in field research is the internal validity of the observed variables which in field settings may be influenced by other factors (Trevino, 1992).

Most of the research designs covered in this book involve laboratory research. Laboratory experiments are considered to have a high degree of external validity if the findings can be generalised to real situations and populations. The external validity of laboratory research can be enhanced by designing experiments that are similar to naturally occurring situations. Moreover, research participants should be representative of real populations rather than homogenous sub-populations such as students. This is where improvement is needed in the experimental designs used in behavioural ethics research. The most commonly used measures – the matrix task, the die experiment, and the dictator game – are not activities that reflect realistic conditions. The characteristics of research participants have improved in the last ten years with most studies including varied samples of participants. Typically, a series of four or five studies are carried out with some of the samples consisting of students and other samples including more heterogeneous participants. Another challenge in laboratory research is the reduction of social desirability bias. This form of bias can be avoided by embedding the experimental task within a set of other, unrelated tasks so that it is harder for the participants to guess the purpose of the study. Social desirability bias can also be reduced by designing experiments in such a way that the participants think their unethical behaviour goes undetected. These practices are however associated with a degree of deception and therefore raise their own ethical concerns (Trevino, 1992).

In behavioural ethics research, the focus has been on measuring unethical or dishonest behaviour to obtain a better understanding of the factors that motivate such deviant behaviour. Research participants are typically given an opportunity and an incentive to behave in an unethical way. In what follows, three experimental designs typically used to measure unethical or prosocial behaviour are described: (1) the matrix task, (2) the die experiment, and (3) the dictator game.

The matrix task

The matrix task has been used in many experiments as a measure of dishonesty. The task consists of a simple mathematical task where participants can earn more money by being dishonest about their performance in the task. The participants are given 20 matrices to solve in a limited amount of time. Each matrix consists of 12 three-digit numbers. The participants are instructed to find two numbers that add up to 10 (e.g. 2.57 and 7.43). The calculations are therefore simple and only require concentration on the task rather than mathematical ability. The participants have an incentive to cheat because their payment depends on the number of matrices solved. The participants are typically paid £1 per matrix. They have an opportunity to cheat because they are asked to check the number of correctly solved matrices themselves and then take a corresponding amount of money from an envelope. The participants are made to think their dishonesty cannot be discovered because they are asked to put the matrix sheet in a recycling bin after they have completed the experiment. The participants do not know that each matrix sheet is unique and can be traced by the researchers because of the set of three-digit numbers in a specific matrix. Researchers have used different measures for dishonesty in the matrix task. One measure is the percentage of participants who cheat in comparison to a control group (e.g. 27%). Another measure is the magnitude of cheating calculated as a mean across the test and control groups (e.g. £4.60).

The die experiment

The die experiment is similar to the matrix task in the sense that it measures dishonesty in a situation where participants can lie to gain a higher payment for participating in the experiment. The participants are asked to roll a die inside a cup and then report the result on a sheet of paper. They are made to think that lying cannot be discovered because no one else can see the result of the die roll. Researchers have used different incentives to encourage cheating. For example, the participants may be paid £1 for 1, £2 for 2, and so on. The participants may also be told that those with the highest die roll score will be entered to a prize draw of different values. Dishonesty is measured as deviance from a statistically probable result. The die experiment is less flexible than the matrix task in the sense that the results are measured across the test and control groups rather than for each participant. It is therefore difficult to include demographic or other individual variables in the experiment. The die experiment is however very quick to run, and it can be run with minimal instructions in a consistent way across different groups of participants. There are variations of the die experiment developed to measure a number of variables in addition to dishonesty.

The dictator game

The dictator game is used to measure pro-social behaviour rather than ethical or unethical behaviour. The participants are given 10 units to distribute between the other participant and themselves. The units normally correspond to money so that 1 unit equals £1. The participants are asked to decide how much money they would give to another participant whose identity they do not know. The participant can keep all the money or give all of it to the other participant. Pro-social behaviour is measured as the amount of money given to the other participant. This amount is normally given as a mean across the test and control groups (e.g. £4.46). On average, participants give away 4 units out of 10. They therefore keep a little more than they give away. Giving money to another participant in the dictator game is against one's self-interest. Because of this, the dictator game measures behaviour that can be described as altruistic. The participants could keep all the money without punishment. The dictator game is therefore often used to measure 'pro-social' or 'charitable' behaviour that goes beyond what is expected.

Summary

In sum, the goal of the behavioural study of ethics is to identify and observe variables that explain and predict people's ethical or unethical behaviour. Research in behavioural ethics involves the development of hypothesis which are tested in laboratory or field settings with the majority of studies being carried out in laboratory conditions. In laboratory designs, participants are given an opportunity and an incentive to cheat while thinking that their behaviour can go unnoticed. Three designs – the matrix task, the die experiment, and the dictator game – have been particularly popular and provide continuity and reliability of research findings across studies. However, the designs can be criticised for being artificial without linkages to real situations and activities that people encounter in their work life or spare time.

Key readings

Rosenbaum, S. M., Billinger, S., and Stieglitz, N. 2014. Let's be honest: A review of experimental evidence of honesty and truth-telling. *Journal of Economic Psychology* 45, 181–196.

The article provides a review of 63 experimental studies about dishonesty and includes a critical assessment of six types of experimental tasks used in these studies. The experimental designs include natural and laboratory settings.

Trevino, L. K. 1992. Experimental approaches to studying ethical-unethical behavior in organizations. *Business Ethics Quarterly* 2 (2), 121–136.

The article consists of a thorough evaluation of the use of experiments in researching ethics. Both laboratory and field experiments are evaluated for their strengths and weaknesses.

Mock assessment questions

- Identify and discuss the main challenges of studying ethics in experimental settings.
- Explain the matrix task and how it differs from the die experiment and the dictator game.

Class exercise

Explain or ask students to perform the matrix task. Then ask students to assess the external validity of the task by identifying three real-life activities that might be similar to the task.

Part II
Individual factors

4   Introduction

Individual qualities and experiences influence how sensitive people are to ethical issues and how they respond to these issues. Historically, research has focused on the impact of age, education, and gender on ethical behaviour, suggesting that older women with certain educational backgrounds are particularly ethical. Research in behavioural ethics has shed new light on the individual factors that play a role in determining behaviour. In this second part of the book, this new research is reviewed as it adds to historical research and creates new areas of research.

5 Are women really more ethical than men?

Learning outcomes

- Identify reasons explaining differences in ethical reasoning between men and women.
- Discuss the principles underpinning the theory of care ethics.

Biological sex is often included as a variable in studies about ethical decision-making and behaviour. The results are however mixed and inconsistent across studies. Women are generally found to be more ethical, but there are also studies where there is no difference between men and women. In a review of 38 studies, women were reported to be more ethical than men in ten of the studies (Craft, 2013). In another review of 29 studies, women were found to be more ethical in 19 studies in comparison to five studies where men were reported to be more ethical (Lehnert et al., 2015). One interesting finding is that sex differences are stronger among student populations in comparison to work populations (Franke et al., 1997; Robin and Babin, 1997). Such findings may be explained by early socialisation which may lead to young men and women having different values and ethical approaches, but these differences disappear as people start working and adapt to organisational roles and practices (Franke et al., 1997). Another set of studies has focused on examining gender as a social-psychological construct in distinction to biological sex (e.g. McCabe et al., 2006). Accordingly, some of the mixed findings may be a result of treating gender as a dichotomous variable rather than a combination of traits and attitudes.

Even though participant gender is typically reported in experimental studies, gender is not often investigated as the main variable. In a study about negotiation ethics, gender was examined as one of the main variables affecting ethical decision-making. The participants consisting of 216 undergraduate students were asked to consider the following scenario:

> You are trying to sell your stereo to raise money for an upcoming trip overseas. The stereo works great and an audiophile friend tells you that if he were in the market for stereo equipment (which he isn't), he'd give you $500 for it. A few days later, the first potential buyer comes to see the stereo. The buyer looks it over and asks a few questions about how it works. You assure the buyer that the stereo works well. When asked how much, you tell the buyer that you already had an offer for $500. They buyer buys the stereo for $550.

The participants were either asked to imagine themselves in the role of the seller or a classmate as the seller in the scenario. They were also asked to indicate the morality of the seller's behaviour on a scale from 1 (strongly disagree) to 7 (strongly agree). On average, men viewed the seller's behaviour as more acceptable than women did (5.47 vs 4.96). Moreover, men viewed the seller's behaviour more acceptable when they put themselves in the position of the seller in comparison to imagining a classmate in the situation (5.88 vs 5.08). Women did not change their view about the acceptability of the seller's behaviour in the self and other condition (4.99 vs 4.92). The researchers argued on this basis that men are not only less ethical than women, but men can also demonstrate more moral hypocrisy.

Researchers have used the matrix task to measure dishonesty among men and women. In one study (Friesen and Gangadharan, 2012), the researchers recruited 115 participants who were asked to find a pair of numbers that added to 10 from a matrix of 12 three-digit numbers (e.g. 3.65 and 6.35). The participants were given altogether 20 matrices to solve in 10 minutes. They had an incentive to cheat because they were told they would get $1 for each matrix they had solved correctly. The participants were able to cheat because they were instructed to pay themselves from an envelope containing cash. The researchers found that the participants solved on average 4.5 matrices. They took on average £2.43 more money than they should have taken on the basis of the matrices they had solved. When the researchers analysed the data for men and women separately, they found that men took more money than women when they were being dishonest. Men took on average 21% of the maximum possible amount while women took 7%. Only one female participant took the maximum amount of money in comparison to nine male participants. Moreover, the magnitude of dishonesty was greater for older and locally born men who found it was acceptable to gain from lying. Women's dishonesty was affected by their aversion to risk with risk averse women taking less money. Overall, men were found to be less ethical than women, and the behaviour of men and women was explained by different factors with women's behaviour being affected by their attitude to risk.

Carol Gilligan, a feminist psychologist, proposed in her well-known book, *In a Different Voice* (1982), that women reason about ethical choices differently from men. Gilligan developed her arguments about female ethics while studying the moral development of children together with Lawrence Kohlberg in the 1960s. Gilligan started her career as a research assistant in Kohlberg's team, but later came to criticise Kohlberg's work because it arguably reflected male values and thinking. Kohlberg proposed on the basis of studying young boys that a sense of morality progresses through six stages with the highest level of moral development consisting of using abstract principles derived from a commitment to justice. Gilligan argued that Kohlberg's theory was a reflection of the moral development of boys and the inability of the predominantly male researcher team to understand and theorise how girls reason about moral dilemmas.

To illustrate her argument, Gilligan (1982) compared the moral reasoning of Jake and Amy, two intelligent and perceptive 11-year-olds. The children were asked to consider a scenario where a man, Heinz, was thinking whether he should steal a medicine that he could not afford to save the life of his wife. Jake was clear that Heinz should steal the medicine because 'a human life is worth more than money'. Jake framed the dilemma as a conflict between the values of property and life where life was more important than property. Jake regarded law as something that had been produced by people and was therefore fallible. In contrast, Amy suggested that instead of stealing the medicine, Heinz should have found another way of obtaining it. Amy was concerned about what would happen to the wife if Heinz was discovered stealing and consequently imprisoned. Because of this, Amy suggested that 'they should really talk it out and find some other way to make the money'. For Amy, the solution to the dilemma was found through working with others. According to Gilligan, Jake saw the dilemma as a logical problem while Amy regarded it as a situation that could be resolved through communication between people.

Researchers from Kohlberg's team assigned a lower value to the reasoning of Amy because of their 'inability to understand her response' and as a result they thought her moral judgement was at a lower level than Jake's. In contrast, Jake's abstraction of the moral problem from its empirical context was seen as an example of a high level of moral reasoning. Gillian however argued that Amy's reasoning demonstrated ethical reasoning based on maintaining social relationships and harmony, which Gilligan referred to as a theory of care ethics. Gilligan's arguments about gender differences in moral reasoning have not been empirically supported (Friedman et al., 1987; Lifton, 1985), but her theory of care ethics has been influential in providing another perspective to ethics and morality. Gilligan's assertion that the theory of moral development is based on studying boys and therefore reflects male values is similar to the increasing number of examples given about how theories and products are developed for men. For example, there are concerns that artificial intelligence is biased against women.

In sum, Carol Gilligan argued that ethical theories reflect male values and reasoning because they have been developed by a body of male academics who have studied male populations, but there is currently little empirical support for this argument. The relationship between gender and ethics has attracted some attention among researchers, but no conclusive findings exist about the effect of gender on ethics. Current findings suggest that men are less ethical than women and they may also be more hypocritical about their behaviour. Gender differences seem to be stronger among younger populations because early socialisation and education may have enhanced gender roles and values, but differences become less important as people enter organisations where they comply with organisational norms and expectations. However, older men may be the least ethical in their behaviour, but this finding needs replication and it is not yet clear why.

Key readings

Gilligan, C. 1982. *In a different voice: Psychological theory and women's development*. Cambridge: Harvard University Press.
In this well-known and influential book, Carol Gilligan presents her theory of ethics of care. Accordingly, women evaluate ethical dilemmas in the context of social relationships that need to be maintained and fostered in comparison to more abstract and formal reasoning pursued by men. Gilligan's arguments in the book draw on interviews with young girls and boys to illustrate the different voice that women have.
Friesen, L., and Gangadharan, L. 2012. Individual level evidence of dishonesty and the gender effect. *Economics Letters* 117, 624–626.
The researchers study both the likelihood and the magnitude of dishonesty using the matrix task. The results show that men are more likely to cheat than women and, when they do so, they also cheat by a larger amount than women.

Mock assessment questions

- Are women more ethical than men?
- What is Gilligan's argument about differences in ethical reasoning between men and women?
- Early socialisation is often presented as a reason for differences between men and women. Give examples of early socialisation that may lead to differences in ethical reasoning between men and women.

Suggested class activity

Ask students to take the moral foundations test online at https://www.idrlabs. com/morality/6/test.php. The test has been developed by Ravi Iyer and Jonathan Haidt. Ask students to note down the percentages they get for each moral core (care, fairness, purity, loyalty, authority, liberty). Then ask which core they would expect to be the strongest for women and which one for men. Ask them to explain why. Then ask students if they are happy to share their personal scores and whether their test results reflected expected gender patterns. If their score did not follow expected trends, ask them to consider why not.

6   Social class and dishonesty

Learning outcomes

- Explain how social class influences ethical behaviour.
- Give examples of how social class can be studied in experiments.

Some of the richest philanthropic foundations in the world have been founded by wealthy individuals from a middle class or higher social class background. The Joseph Rowntree Charitable Trust was founded by Joseph Rowntree whose middle class family was in the groceries business. The Bill and Melinda Gates Foundation was established by Bill Gates whose father was a lawyer and mother served on several boards of directors. All of these philanthropists used their influence and resources to enhance the quality of housing, education, and health in society. There are also other historical and current philanthropists who have made significant charitable contributions. Based on these anecdotal examples, one might be tempted to argue that people from higher social classes act in socially responsible and benevolent ways. Recent research in experimental psychology however suggests that Bill Gates and Joseph Rowntree may be outliers and people from higher social classes have a tendency to behave in self-interested and unethical ways when compared to people from other social classes.

In a study about driving behaviour in California (Piff et al., 2012), researchers sent observers to record the conduct of drivers at a busy intersection. The observers at the intersection took notes about the make, age, and appearance of vehicles to determine the social class of drivers. The vehicles and their drivers were then classified into five categories from the lowest to the highest social class. It had been previously discovered that vehicle type is a good predictor of social class (Frank, 1999). In addition to vehicle type, the observers also noted whether the drivers cut off in front of other vehicles when they were waiting to turn. The researchers observed a total of 274 turns at the intersection. From among these turns, drivers cut in front of other drivers in 12.4% of the cases. Almost a third (30%) of the drivers coming from the highest social class cut off another driver when turning. This percentage was over twice as high as the percentage of drivers from the next social class. When the researchers carried out a similar study about drivers cutting off pedestrians at a zebra crossing, 34.9% performed the act with the percentages varying from 0% in the lowest social class category to almost 50% in the highest social class category. Driving behaviour therefore indicates that people from higher social classes are less likely to comply with driving regulations than people from lower social classes.

Driving may be a special context in which social class is particularly important for explaining unethical behaviour. In order to understand whether social class predicts unethical behaviour in other contexts, Piff et al. (2012) asked participants in a laboratory setting to roll a die for five times on a virtual platform. The participants performed the task online and were told that they should report the total of the five rolls to a laboratory assistant. They were also told that a higher overall total would increase their chance of winning a cash prize. The computer programme they were using had however been set to produce a total of 12 from the five die rolls performed by each participant. If the participants reported a total that was higher than 12, the researchers knew they were lying. The researchers also asked the participants to answer survey questions about their social status and attitudes towards greed. They found that both social class and positive attitudes towards greed were associated with cheating. When both factors were entered into a linear regression model, only attitudes towards greed, however, predicted lying. The researchers concluded from these results that upper class people have more positive views about greed, which explains why their behaviour is less ethical than the behaviour of their peers from lower social classes.

Extant research therefore suggests that social class and unethical behaviour are connected. More research needs to be carried out about the factors that explain this relationship, but based on current research, attitudes to greed are one factor that underpin the relationship between social class and unethical behaviour. There may also be other factors that have not been investigated yet. When it comes to the donations of wealthy philanthropists from a higher social class, other factors or psychological mechanisms may be at play in explaining their pro-social behaviour.

Key readings

Piff, P. K., Stancato, D. M., Cote, S., Mendoza-Denton, R., and Keltner, D. 2012. Higher social class predicts increased unethical behavior. *PNAS* 109 (11), 4086–4091.
Seven separate studies published in a prestigious journal demonstrate that individuals from higher social classes are consistently less ethical than individual from lower social classes. The experiments combine natural settings and laboratory designs.

Mock assessment questions

- Do you think driving behaviour is a good indicator of other forms of ethical or unethical behaviour? Why? Why not?
- Bill Gates has donated large sums of money for charitable causes. Do you think he complies with driving regulations?

Suggested class activity

Ask students to identify the three most ethical people they know and the three least ethical people they know without naming the individuals. Then ask them to indicate which social class they come from, using a scale from 1 to 5 with 1 being the lowest and 5 the highest. Discuss with the whole class whether patterns exist regarding the social class of the most and least ethical people they know.

7 Sense for fairness increases whistleblowing

Learning outcomes

- Explain how a sense of fairness and a sense of loyalty interact to produce whistleblowing.
- Recommend measures that organisations can take to increase whistleblowing.

Chelsea Manning is one of the most famous whistleblowers of the 21st century. Manning was an intelligence analyst working for the US Armed Forces in Iraq. In 2010, she downloaded nearly 750,000 documents including military reports, diplomatic cables, and video material from army databases to bring attention to what she considered were war crimes. She initially sought to share the documents with the *Washington Post* and the *New York Times*, but ended up sending them to WikiLeaks after the newspapers showed little interest for the material. The documents included sensitive and classified materials relating to US action in Iraq including the murder of Reuters journalists and bombing of civilian targets. Manning was subsequently captured and charged in the US for espionage, theft, and computer fraud. She was sentenced to 35 years in a maximum security prison, but President Obama later commuted the sentence and Manning was released in 2017. Manning's case highlights the rareness of whistleblowing. She was one of thousands of people working for the US Army in Iraq and the only one – as far as the public knows – to share documents with an outside body to raise concerns about the activities of the US Armed Forces in the country. As a military analyst, Manning had better access than many others to sensitive documents, but her close colleagues and other army personnel with similar access decided not to take action. Why did Manning blow the whistle when others did not?

One stream of research in psychology suggests that the values held by people make them more or less likely to report wrongdoing (Waytz et al., 2013). From among the set of basic moral values held by people, it is the values of fairness and loyalty that explain why some people are likelier than others to blow the whistle. As moral values, fairness refers to the treatment of individuals and groups in an equal way, whereas loyalty is defined as the preferential treatment of some individuals over others because of personal closeness or a membership to a group. Both values can be found in very young children and also in some primates. For example, children expect resources to be shared fairly between individuals by the age of two. Some of the negative reactions against whistleblowers arise from the expectation that people do feel and express loyalty towards the communities and organisations they belong to. There are many situations where the values of fairness and loyalty conflict and it is their relative strength that determines the choices individual people make. For example, people with a strong sense of fairness would hesitate less than those with a strong sense of loyalty to report a crime by a family member to authorities. Those with a strong sense of fairness are also likelier to consider ethical decision situations from a less involved perspective than those who feel a strong sense of loyalty towards another person or a group.

Researchers have studied the impact of the values of fairness and loyalty on whistleblowing through surveys that include questions about hypothetical situations. In a study, Waytz et al. (2013) asked participants questions about fairness and loyalty and calculated a composite score based on the relative importance of the two values in participant answers. The participants were then asked how likely they were to blow the whistle about various unethical practices. They were also asked about their likelihood of blowing the whistle for perpetrators of various levels of closeness to them from strangers to family members. The results showed that the stronger the sense of fairness in relation to a sense of loyalty, the more likely the participants were to blow the whistle. Furthermore, people in the experiment were more likely to report the wrongdoing of a stranger than a family member. Measured on a scale from 1 to 7 with 7 indicating the highest likelihood of blowing the whistle, the willingness to blow the whistle was the highest for strangers (M=5.32) and acquaintances (M=5.02) and the lowest for friends (M=4.48) and family members (M=4.27). The relationship between values and whistleblowing was the strongest for relatively minor ethical transgressions like spraying graffiti and cheating and the weakest for more serious offences such as stabbing. The researchers therefore concluded that once an issue is perceived as very serious, the sense of loyalty or fairness does not affect the decision to blow the whistle.

The same researchers (Waytz et al., 2013) found that whistleblowing can be evoked by reminding people about their sense of fairness and justice. The researchers run an experiment in which they divided the participants into two groups and asked the first group to write about why fairness is important among co-workers, while the other group was asked to write about the importance of loyalty. All the participants were then asked to carry out a typing task. In this task, they were asked to write in words the numbers from 1 to 30. They were also told that they would see the work of the previous participant. This work contained multiple mistakes and was clearly sub-standard. Once the participants had finished the task, they were asked a number of questions about the task including questions about the work of the previous participant, giving them an opportunity to report the work as unacceptable and block the participant from future studies. The results showed that those who had written about the importance of fairness were likelier to report the work of the previous participant as unacceptable than those who had written about loyalty (4.36 versus 3.72 on a scale from 1 to 5). These findings suggest that being reminded about a value, whether fairness or loyalty, can influence whistleblowing behaviour making it more or less likely. It is therefore possible in organisations to encourage whistleblowing by stressing the importance of fairness in internal communication.

Research shows that the values of fairness and loyalty play an important role in whistleblowing decisions with a sense of fairness being associated with enhanced whistleblowing and a sense of loyalty making whistleblowing less likely (Waytz et al., 2013). The importance of loyalty in whistleblowing decisions may explain some of the cultural differences in whistleblowing (Waytz et al., 2013). Whistleblowing is seen as more ethical in individualistic countries such as the US and less ethical in collectivist countries such as Japan where loyalty is an essential part of the culture (Brody et al., 1998). The importance of loyalty also explains why there are repercussions against whistleblowers who may be seen as traitors, especially if whistleblowing leads to reputational or other forms of damage for the whistleblower's group. The nature of wrongdoing is also important for predicting whistleblowing. When the moral transgression is perceived as not very serious (e.g. taking office supplies for personal use), the relative importance of the value of fairness versus the value of loyalty is particularly important in explaining whether individuals choose to report the wrongdoing. When the moral transgression is more serious (e.g. product defect leading to physical harm), the values of fairness and loyalty have a weaker influence on whistleblowing decisions. Finally, organisations can encourage whistleblowing by activating a sense of fairness among its employees through relatively simple measures such as statements about the importance compliance with regulations.

Whistleblowing is sometimes presented as something that is beneficial for organisations and the society, but detrimental for the whistleblower. Organisations benefit from whistleblowing because it alerts them to malpractice that may have a negative impact on performance and reputation. The society benefits from whistleblowing because wrongdoing can have a serious impact on people's health and wellbeing. Whistleblowers themselves may however experience negative consequences from raising an alarm or taking action in other ways. For example, Edward Snowden who leaked documents to journalists about large-scale, unlawful surveillance ended up living in exile in Russia. The high profile cases of Manning, Snowden, and others are likely to make whistleblowers think carefully about the consequences of bringing attention to organisational wrongdoing.

Key readings

Waytz, A., Dungan, J., and Young, L. 2013. The whistleblower's dilemma and the fairness-loyalty tradeoff. *Journal of Experimental Social Psychology* 49, 1027–1033.

A series of four studies demonstrate the trade-off between fairness and loyalty to explain whistleblowing decisions. The studies involve both hypothetical and real whistleblowing scenarios. The studies show that a sense of fairness makes whistleblowing more likely and this sense can be activated through various prompts.

Graham, J., Haidt, J., and Nosek, B.A. 2009. Liberals and conservatives rely on different sets of moral foundations. *Journal of Personality and Social Psychology* 96 (5), 1029–1046.

The researchers demonstrate in four studies that liberals are particularly influenced by concerns over fairness and harm, while conservatives are affected by a broader range of moral values. The difference helps to explain why liberals and conservatives disagree on moral topics and may have different views about, for example, whistleblowing.

Mock assessment question

- How do the values of fairness and loyalty interact to produce whistleblowing in relation to different kinds of moral transgressions?
- What measures can organisations take to encourage whistleblowing?

Suggested class activity

Show the students Frans de Waal's video about monkeys that are paid unequally: https://www.youtube.com/watch?v=meiU6TxysCg. Ask students the following questions:

- How does whistleblowing take place in the video?
- How do you think the sense of fairness may have developed in monkeys?
- In what conditions would the monkey not throw the food back?

8   Self-reflection and moral balancing make people more ethical

Learning outcomes

- Distinguish the two components of the concept of moral equilibrium.
- Explain how the idea of moral equilibrium relates to one's self-concept.

The idea of moral equilibrium first featured when researchers noted that participants in laboratory experiments were more responsive to help requests when they had performed unpleasant tasks in laboratory experiments. In one instance, research participants had applied painful electric shocks to other participants during an experiment. These same participants seemed to compensate for the electric shocks by agreeing to help researchers when asked to do so. There was a clear difference between the participants who had executed shocks and those who had only observed others applying electric shocks. The researchers suspected the participants who had applied electric shocks were more responsive to help requests to compensate for the behaviour that had lowered their sense of self-worth during experiments (Carlsmith and Gross, 1969). A comparable situation from everyday life is when a family member surprises others by doing something nice like cooking a dinner or buying flowers, which may seem suspicious to others who react by asking: 'What (bad) have you done now?'

People internalise norms and moral values as they grow up in a particular family and social environment. The norms and values then serve as a benchmark for assessing their own behaviour. A person can feel uncomfortable if their behaviour diverts from their internal standards. Brain imaging studies show that the same areas of the brain are activated when people comply with internal norms as when they receive an external reward such as food or money (De Quervain et al.,

2004). Researchers (Mazar et al., 2008) have argued that the norms and values are connected to how people perceive themselves, their self-concept, and people alter their behaviour to maintain a positive self-concept. When faced with ethical decision situations, people can feel conflicted between pursuing their self-interest and maintaining a positive self-image. In some situations, people forego financial or other benefits in order to comply with their internal values and to maintain a positive self-concept. For example, an individual may be tempted not to report all their income to tax authorities, but they decide to be honest in order to keep a positive image of themselves as a law-abiding citizen. In other situations, people find a different balance between pursuing a self-interest and keeping a positive self-image. For example, a person might not donate to an environmental charity because they believe they recycle more than other people.

The dilemma between self-interest and ethical behaviour has been conceptualised as moral licensing. Accordingly, a virtuous act gives people a licence to behave in a selfish and unethical way. In contrast, people are less likely to regulate their ethical behaviour after a good deed has given them a moral boost. Two researchers (Mazar and Zhong, 2010) investigated the phenomenon of moral licensing in the context of green shopping. They conducted an experiment with 90 participants who were each seated at a desk with a computer terminal and an envelope containing five Canadian dollars in different denominations. In the control condition, the participants were asked to select purchases in a conventional online store which had nine conventional products and three green products. In the experimental condition, the participants chose purchases in a green online store with three conventional products and nine green products. The products and the prices were the same in both online stores. After finishing the task, the participants were asked to complete another task involving 90 rounds of decisions about the placing of dots on a computer screen. They were told that the computer screen would be split diagonally and 20 dots would be scattered across the line. Their task was to press a key to show which side – left or right – had more dots. The dots were distributed so that it was clear which side had more dots. The participants earned money for each time there were more dots on the right side of the diagonal line. The researchers however knew that in 40% of the rounds the dots would be on the right-hand side. At the end of the task, the participants could see the amount of money they had earned on the screen and they were instructed to pay themselves from the envelope on the desk. The researchers found that the participants from the control condition had seen the dots on the right-hand side of the diagonal line in 42.5% of the rounds, which was not statistically different from the correct 40% of the rounds. The participants who had been in the green shopping condition had pressed the right-hand side key in 51.4% of the trials. Dishonest pressing of the key was therefore more prevalent in the group that had shopped in the green online store before the visual task. The researchers also found that these participants paid themselves more than the participants in the other condition. The overpayments were on average $0.56 in comparison to $0.08 among the participants in the control group. The researchers concluded that shopping ethically gave the participants a licence to pursue their self-interest in the dot task.

In another experiment, researchers (Sachdeva et al., 2009) studied whether moral licensing exists in parallel to the opposite process of moral cleansing. As well as feeling entitled to behave less ethically, people may also behave especially ethically to compensate for previous moral transgressions and in this way maintain a positive self-concept. In the experiment, the participants were asked to copy a list of nine words and write a story about themselves that included the nine words. The participants were using words that were either neutral, positive, or negative. For example, positive words included the words of caring, generous, and fair, while the negative words included the words of greedy, mean, and selfish. The participants were then asked to play the role of a manager at a manufacturing plant. The plant was releasing pollutants to the air, but managers of similar plants had collectively made a commitment to use filters 60% of the time at a cost of $1.2 million. The participants were asked at which interval between 0% and 100% they would run the filters with each interval costing $0.2m million. The findings showed that the participants exposed to the negative word condition ran the filters 73% of the time and were therefore using the filter beyond the general commitment of 60% among managers. Participants in the positive word condition were less likely to run the filters at 56% of the time and below the common commitment of 60%. The experiment suggests that moral regulation works towards an equilibrium where people compensate for negative associations by engaging in pro-social behaviours beyond the norm and feel licensed to do less than the norm after feeling good about themselves. The experiment also suggests that moral regulation does not only apply to individual acts of shopping or charitable donations, but it also relates to behaviour in work roles.

The awareness people have about their moral standards varies from one person and situation to another. When people are mindful about their moral standards, they are likelier to consider any decision or action in relation to the moral standards, but there may be situations where they are less aware of their moral standards. For example, they may be in such a hurry that they are not very self-aware. Researchers (Mazar et al., 2008) have studied whether reminding people about moral standards increases self-awareness and therefore more ethical behaviour so that a positive self-concept can be maintained. The researchers recruited 229 students to participate to an experiment about moral awareness. The participants were allocated to a control group and an experimental group. In the control group, they were asked to write down the names of ten books they had read in high school. In the experimental group, the participants were instructed to list the Ten Commandments. The purpose of the task was to draw the attention of the participants to their moral standards, irrespective of their religion or cultural background, because the researchers expected that the Ten Commandments would make people more aware of moral standards regardless of their personal beliefs. The participants were then asked to carry out the matrix task which gives them an opportunity to gain a higher pay for the experiment by exaggerating the number of matrices they solve when reporting their results. The researchers found that the participants resolved on average 3.1 matrices in both groups. Participants in the book group lied about their performance by reporting that they had resolved an average of 4.2 matrices, while participants in the Ten Commandments group reported that they had resolved 2.8 matrices. The Ten Commandments task had therefore made the participants more ethical and prevented them from lying. The researchers concluded that the Ten Commandments task increased attention on moral standards and this is why no cheating took place in the group that had been asked to list the Ten Commandments.

Based on current research, people engage in moral regulation to maintain a positive self-image and a moral equilibrium they are comfortable with. When they have behaved in virtuous ways, they can feel entitled to behave less ethically. This process is referred to as moral licensing. In contrast, when people seek to boost their self-concept, they engage in moral cleansing by behaving ethically or in virtuous ways. The process of moral cleansing is beneficial for society, but moral licensing can in some situations have detrimental consequences for others. The challenge for organisations is therefore to encourage moral cleansing and prevent moral licensing. One way to do this is to remind people about their moral standards by drawing attention to them, which can make people more ethical because they seek to maintain a positive self-image.

Key readings

Sachdeva, S., Iliev, R., and Medin, D. L. 2009. Sinning saints and saintly sinners: The paradox of moral self-regulation. *Psychological Science* 20 (4), 523–528.
Three studies demonstrate how one's self-concept is connected to ethical behaviour through moral licensing and cleansing. One of the studies shows that moral regulation only takes place when one's own behaviour is concerned, not when others are being observed or when their behaviour is assessed.
Mazar, N., and Zhong, C.-B. 2010. Do green products make us better people? *Psychological Science* 21 (4), 494–498.
Three experimental studies show that exposure to green products and the experience of buying green products have different behavioural consequences. While exposure to green products makes people less selfish, purchasing green products leads to more selfish behaviour.

Mock assessment questions

- Explain the concept of moral equilibrium and the two main processes linked to it.
- Give three examples of moral licensing from real life or experimental studies.

Suggested class activity

Show students the Ethics Unwrapped video produced by the University of Texas about the concept of moral equilibrium: https://ethicsunwrapped.utexas. edu/video/moral-equilibrium. Ask students for examples from their personal life about moral licensing and moral compensation.

9   Are we creatively dishonest?

Learning outcomes

- Explain why creativity increases unethical behaviour.
- Give examples of how creativity can be prompted in people with an influence on their ethical behaviour.

Creative people are celebrated across professional fields as leaders and change-makers who have the courage, discipline, and vision to challenge old practices and invent something new. Creativity refers to the development of new and usable ideas that are often based on divergent or unconventional thinking (Amabile, 1983). Challenging established wisdom and thinking differently has led to many innovations that have been beneficial for business and society. Creativity has been especially valued in industries where new technologies provide opportunities for start-ups to challenge more established companies. Creativity has also been important in cultural industries including performing arts, fashion, and the media. Recent research however suggests that creativity may have a darker side. The negative side of creativity is illustrated by examples of highly creative people who have ignored the usual rules of acceptable behaviour. For example, Steve Jobs drove his car without a licence plate and parked on a slot reserved for disabled drivers (Vincent and Kouchaki, 2016). In the same way, one of the founders of Uber, Travis Kalanick, was forced to step down from his role as the chief executive of the company after being accused of bullying and sexual harassment. Is it possible that these examples of unethical behaviour by creative people are a sign of the dark side of creativity? Does creativity come with the cost of entitled and unethical behaviour?

In one study, Gino and Ariely (2012) researched employees in an advertising agency to explore whether there is a relationship between creativity and dishonesty. They obtained data through an online questionnaire about 99 employees across 17 different departments in the agency. The employees were asked ten questions about ethically questionable behaviours and how likely they were to engage in these behaviours. For example, one of the questions was about inflating business expense reports and another about taking office supplies home from work. The researchers then calculated a composite value that represented an employee's likelihood of engaging in unethical behaviours. The researchers also asked the employees and three senior managers how much creativity was required in the 19 different departments. The findings showed that self-reported dishonesty was connected to creativity required on the job. The relationship was particularly strong when creativity was assessed by managers. The Pearson correlation co-efficient for this relationship was 0.46, meaning that the departmental creativity rating by managers explained 46% of variance in dishonesty.

The study carried out among the employees of an advertising agency showed that creative people are likelier to engage in unethical behaviour, but it did not explain why creativity increases unethical behaviour. In another study, Gino and Ariely (2012) sought to replicate their original findings in a more controlled setting and explore what factors explain the relationship between creativity and unethical behaviour. They measured creativity by asking participants to take the Remote Association Test consisting of word associations. In the test, the participants are given three words and asked to find another word that logically connects the three words. For example, the word 'cold' connects the words 'sore', 'shoulder', and 'seat'. The participants were then asked to roll a die. They were told that they would be paid on the basis of the die roll with $1 for 1, $2 for 2, and finally $6 for 6. The participants therefore had a monetary incentive to achieve a high die outcome. In the control condition, the participants were asked to roll the die once inside a cup and report the result on a collection slip. In the experimental condition, the participants were asked to roll the die several times to ensure it was legitimate, but still report the result of the first die. Previous research had shown that allowing participants to roll a die several times gives them a justification to lie and report the highest die result rather than the first one (Shalvi et al., 2012). The researchers found that creative people reported higher die results in the condition where the participants were asked to roll the die only once. When the participants were asked the roll the die several times, there was no difference in the reported die results. The findings suggest that creative people are less ethical in settings where no easy justifications are available for dishonesty. When such a justification exists like it did in the multiple die condition, creative people are as likely as others to cheat. The findings suggest that creative people are less ethical because they are better at finding justifications for unethical behaviour.

Another pair of researchers, Vincent and Kouchaki (2016), investigated whether the relationship between creativity and dishonesty could be explained by other factors. They were particularly interested in finding out whether creativity can give rise to a sense of entitlement which leads to self-interested and unethical behaviour. They invited experimental participants to take the Remote Association Test in which participants received an automatically generated message after seven rounds. The purpose of the message was to alter the perception of the rarity of creativity. In the rare condition, the participants received a message saying that: 'Creativity is rare. You performed very well on this activity, which many people do not'. In the common condition, the participants were told that: 'Creativity is common. You participated very well on this activity, which many people do'. In the final, control condition, the participants were told that: 'The previous activity measures how people find connections among seemingly unconnected ideas or words. You performed very well on this activity'. The participants were then asked to engage in a decision-making activity in which they were able to earn more money than a partner by lying. More specifically, they were able to send one out of two messages to a partner. The first message was a lie about how much money the partner would earn. Instead of earning $5, the partner would earn $2. The second message was true and meant the partner could earn $5. The participants had an incentive to send the first message because they would have earned more from sending it ($5 versus $2). The participants were then asked questions about psychological entitlement and creativity identity. The findings showed that participants in the rare identity condition felt a higher level of entitlement (4.18) than participants in the common creativity condition (3.56) or the control condition (3.41). In terms of dishonesty, the participants in the rare creativity condition were over twice as likely to lie as participants in the common creativity condition or the control condition (86% versus 40%/32%). The researchers also carried out further statistical tests to establish that when creativity is perceived as rare, it causes a sense of entitlement which leads to unethical behaviour.

Researchers have also explored whether it is possible to activate creativity in a temporary way with the same detrimental effect on ethical behaviour. In one experiment (Gino and Ariely, 2012), participants consisting of 111 students in the US received a show-up fee of $4 and a further $10 on the basis of their performance in the experiment.

All the participants were asked to form 20 grammatically correct sentences from groups of five words. In order to trigger creativity in some of the participants, the researchers asked the participants to formulate sentences from words associated with creativity including 'originality' and 'imagination'. In the control group, the participants were instructed to form sentences from random words not related to creativity such as 'sky' and 'why'. The participants were then asked to carry out another two tasks. The first task was the Duncan Candle Problem that measures creativity. The participants were shown a picture of a candle, a pack of matches, and a box of tacks on a table. They were asked how they would use the objects on the table to attach the candle to a wall so that it burned without dripping wax on the table or the floor. The correct answer is to use the box that holds the tacks in an unusual way as a candleholder and attach the box to the wall. The percentage of participants who solved the candle task was higher in the creative group than in the control group (47% versus 27%), meaning that those who had been asked to form sentences from words related to creativity became more creative during the candle task. In order to measure ethical behaviour, the researchers asked the participants to carry out the matrix task which provides an opportunity for the participants to cheat when they report their results for the test. The percentage of participants who overstated their performance was clearly higher in the creative group (49%) than in the control group (27%). The results of the experiment show that a creative mind-set increases unethical behaviour even when it is artificially evoked in people.

To conclude, research shows that creativity increases unethical behaviour. The connection between creativity and unethical behaviour goes beyond a creative personality and can be activated temporarily in any group of people. Based on existing research, there are two explanations for why creativity increases unethical behaviour. First, unethical behaviour increases because creativity enables people to find justifications for their self-interested behaviour. Second, unethical behaviour increases because the rarity of creativity makes people feel entitled to behave unethically in self-interested ways. However, as Vincent and Kouchaki (2016) note, creativity does not always lead to unethical behaviour. Current research has been carried out in situations where the participants have had an incentive to be dishonest. Also, creativity is not always rare in organisations and even when it is, it may not be celebrated or perceived as something rare, which means that the link to unethical behaviour may disappear. Vincent and Kouchaki give the example of Google where creativity is an important value and many employees are creative.

Key readings

Gino, F., and Ariely, D. 2012. The dark side of creativity: Original thinkers can be more dishonest. *Journal of Personality and Social Psychology* 102 (3), 445–459.

In this well-known article, the authors show that creativity increases unethical behaviour. Several experiments show that this relationship is explained by the use of creative mindset to find justifications for unethical behaviour. The authors focus on creativity ability and flexibility in thinking.

Vincent, L. C., and Kouchaki, M. 2016. Creative, rare, entitled, and dishonest: How commonality of creativity in one's group decreases and individual's entitlement and dishonesty. *Academy of Management Journal* 59 (4), 1451–1473.

The researchers run a set of experiments to show that rarity of creativity leads to a sense of entitlement which increases unethical behaviour. The concept of creativity used by the authors relates to creative identity rather than creative flexibility.

Mock assessment questions

- What psychological interactions explain the negative impact of creativity on ethical behaviour?
- Explain the difference between creative personality and creative thinking. Give an example of how each can be studied in an experimental setting and how this influences ethical behaviours.

Suggested class activity

Ask students to resolve the following three sets of the Remote Association Test word puzzles by identifying a word that connects three words. For example, the word 'cold' connects the words 'sore', 'shoulder', and 'seat'. The three sets of words are: cream/skate/water, room/blood/salts, and age/mile/sand. Once the students have completed the task, ask for solutions for each set of three words. Take a vote of hands if the students think the test is a good measure for creativity. Ask two students from each side of the argument to share their views.

Part III

Situational factors

10 Introduction

One of the main findings of behavioural ethics research is that individual behaviour is malleable and changes in different situations. The Milgram studies and the Stanford Prison experiment already suggested that social and organisational influences may have a more important impact on behaviour than individual factors. The third part of the book focuses on such situational factors that influence how people behave. Situational factors cover a variety of influences from social norms to more specific elements of the environment in which people live and work, including exposure to cues about wealth and anonymity.

11 We comply with peer norms in good and bad

Learning outcomes

- Explain how social norms and social learning influence ethical behaviour.
- Recommend how ethical behaviour can be encouraged through the enforcement of social norms.

Siemens, a German engineering firm, pleaded guilty in 2008 to making corrupt payments to secure contracts around the world. Over time, as the investigation to the scandal unfolded, it became apparent that corruption and knowledge about it was rife within certain management levels and it had become the norm within the company. There were rooms of cash at certain Siemens offices that could be accessed by managers who then used the cash to make illicit payments. In one occasion, managers had flown with a budget airline, easyJet, carrying millions of Euros with them to make bribes to officials in Italy (Schubert and Miller, 2008). When one manager was interviewed about the scandal later on, he continued to be unable to detach himself from the corrupt culture and saw his behaviour as contributing to the company and its global success (https://www.youtube.com/watch?v=c5lYU_-W9SA). The corruption scandal of Siemens is an example of how unethical norms become adopted and spread within organisations.

In the work context, social norms are often learned through the observation of organisational leaders and peers. The idea of social learning was introduced by Bandura (1965) who proposed that norms are internalised through personal experiences and the observation of others. Research in social identification (Tajfel, 1982) suggests that when people identify with a group, they are particularly influenced by the norms of the group in order to sustain their membership and identity as a group member. People are generally attracted to groups that help them to maintain a positive self-image including groups perceived as ethical (van Prooijen and Ellemers, 2015). Moreover, when group members are perceived as immoral, people avoid these members because the immorality is seen as a threat to the group's image (Brambilla et al., 2013).

The influence of social norms on ethical behaviour has often been studied from two perspectives. The first involves the study of 'bad apples' and their impact on the ethical behaviour of others. The second perspective concerns the examination of positive examples and practices including ethical leadership, codes of conduct, and ethical training programmes. Below, experiments in social norms and learning are discussed in the categories of 'the good' and 'the bad'.

The bad: the rotten apple and its impact

Those of us who eat apples know that one rotten apple can quickly contaminate other apples that also start to decay. If the rotten apple is removed early, the other apples are not affected and remain fresh. Do rotten individuals contaminate others in the same way in the work place? Research suggests that unethical employees do influence the behaviour of others, but the influence is not straightforward.

One study showed that people alter their behaviour depending on whether they identify with the person whose behaviour they observe (Gino et al., 2009a). If the person being observed is part of the same ingroup, people imitate the observed behaviour. In contrast, if the person is from another group, they distance themselves from the person through their behaviour. In the study, participants were randomly divided into four groups and asked to perform the matrix task. All the participants were asked to pay themselves from a brown envelope by moving money to a white envelope. The first group was the control group where participants were asked to give their test to an experimenter who calculated how many matrices had been solved correctly and checked that the participants had left the correct money in the white envelope. In the second condition, the participants were asked to count the number of matrices they solved, write this number on a collection slip, walk to a shredder, and shred their worksheet. The participants were then asked to return the white envelope to a cardboard box without any interference from the experimenter. The participants were therefore able to misreport how many matrices they had solved. Indeed, the results suggested that the participants in the shredder condition cheated more than the participants in the control condition by reporting that they had solved 50% more matrices than the participants in the control group.

The interest of the researchers was however in studying how people react to the unethical behaviour of others. The third and fourth conditions were therefore identical to the second condition except that a professional actor was asked to stand up soon after the participants had started solving matrices and say: 'I've solved everything. What should I do?' It was clear to the other participants that it wasn't possible to solve all the matrices in such a short time and the actor was therefore lying. The difference between the third and the fourth conditions was that in the third condition the actor wore a t-shirt from the university the participants were from, while in the fourth group he wore a t-shirt from another, competitor university. When the actor wore a t-shirt from the same university with the participants, cheating increased to similar levels with the shredder condition. When the actor wore a t-shirt from a different university, cheating decreased to levels slightly higher than in the control group. The experiment suggests that people do not just change their behaviour in alignment with the behaviour of people around them. Instead, if their peers from their in-group behave unethically, they imitate this behaviour, but if the unethical behaviour is carried out by someone from an out-group, they distinguish themselves by becoming more ethical.

In another study (Gino et al., 2009b), the researchers investigated whether the presence of others influences how we respond to unethical behaviour. They studied what happens if people observe unethical behaviour in the presence of in-group members in comparison to out-group members. The researchers invited participants who were all from the University of North Carolina (UNC) to take part in the dictator game. Each participant was given an envelope with $10 and asked to take the money they wanted to keep from the envelope and the rest would be donated to another participant. There were two experimental conditions. In one condition, the participants witnessed the unethical behaviour of an actor who wore a UNC t-shirt. The actor spread the money from the envelope on his desk and said to himself, 'I'm taking everything'. In the other condition, the actor wore a t-shirt from another university, Duke, but otherwise followed the same process. The participants saw the behaviour of the actor because they were seated next to him during the experiment and the seats were placed so that the participants saw each other and what they were wearing. Moreover, in one condition there were two other actors with an UNC t-shirt and in a further condition two actors with a Duke t-shirt. The results showed that when out-group members were present to witness the unethical behaviour, participants left more money than when the other witnesses were from the same university as the participants ($6.03 versus $2.73).

The researchers hence found that the donations made by participants decreased when only in-group members were present during the experiment and increased when out-group members witnessed the unethical behaviour. This suggests that being observed by out-group members makes people more self-aware and reflective of their decisions and may trigger a feeling of guilt. As a result, people take responsibility for the actions of their in-group members and compensate for their behaviour by becoming more ethical themselves. Unlike in the previous experiment about cheating, observing a peer from the same in-group being unethical made the participants more rather than less ethical. The researchers referred to this phenomenon as the contagion or restitution effect caused by bad apples.

The good: the force of positive example

Ideally, ethical behaviour is the norm. Research however shows that people need to be reminded about ethical norms in order to behave ethically. In a study involving 270 customer service representatives, Jerald Greenberg (2002) investigated how an ethics programme influences behaviour. The participants to the study were asked to fill in a survey and pay themselves for their participation from a bowl that contained pennies. An experimenter added some pennies to the bowl from his pocket in the front of the participants to create the illusion he didn't know how many pennies the bowl contained, even though he knew exactly how much money was in the bowl. The experimenter then left the participants alone in the room to pay themselves. Afterwards, the experimenter counted the money to check whether the participants had cheated and paid themselves too much. Prior to the study, some of the participants had received at least ten hours of ethics training consisting of role plays, cases studies, and a summary of how to report unethical conduct in the company. The participants stole significantly less when they had received ethics training (USD 6.24 versus USD 9.99). The researcher concluded that ethical norms need to be made salient to enhance ethical behaviour and reduce unethical behaviour. In the experiment, this had taken place through ethics training.

The presence of others can enhance ethical behaviour. An example of this kind of social control was provided in an experiment run by Kroher and Wolbring (2015). In the experiment, participants were asked to roll a dice either alone in private or in the presence of another participant that introduced an element of social control to the experiment. All the participants were asked to roll the dice twice and record the result on a computer programme. The participants could therefore misreport the result of the die and this was encouraged by differentiated payments for different die results. When the participants rolled a dice in the presence of another participant, they could see each other rolling and reporting the result of the die on a computer screen, although they were instructed not to discuss anything with the other participant. The researchers found that the participants rolling the dice alone reported results that earned them EUR 0.98 more than the participants who rolled the dice in groups of two, but this result only applied to the first die roll, not the second one. For the second die roll, there was no difference between those who rolled the dice alone and those who did it in the presence of others. The analysis of the results suggested that the paired players started to report dishonest results in teams rather than independently from each other. The researchers said it is possible that this phenomenon was caused by participants feeling that they should be earning the same amount from the experiment as their team member, but this suggestion could not be confirmed. What is known is that being in the presence of others reduced cheating when the teams first got together, but this control quickly eroded.

Groups respond more robustly to dishonest behaviour than individuals when the dishonest behaviour is carried out by an out-group. In a study by Keck (2014), experimental participants were allocated to an individual decision condition or to a group of three members who were instructed to discuss each choice they made during the experiment. The participants took part in a game where they could earn money by correctly guessing a number between 0 and 1000. They were told that they would get information from another player, but the player had an incentive to lie because a wrong guess from the participants would increase the payment for the other player. The participants still tended to choose the number given to them because it was the only piece of information they had about the correct number. All the participants were however given the same incorrect number in a message saying: 'The correct number is: X.' After submitting their guess, the participants were told the correct number at which point they realised the other player had given them incorrect information. The participants were then given an opportunity to punish the other player by reducing some of their own pay-off for participating in the experiment. They could spend between EUR 0.10 and EUR 1 to lower the sender's payment by four times the amount spent. The participants were also asked to rate the negative affect they felt towards the other player by responding to six questions on a seven-point scale. The results showed that groups punished the other player more than individual players

(0.40 versus 0.15 euros). The results further showed that negative affect was significantly higher among group members than individuals and mediated the higher penalty applied by the groups. The experiment suggests that groups are more likely to penalise dishonest behaviour than individuals, even when this penalty carries a cost for the group. The use of punitive measures is explained by the negative feeling triggered by out-groups that violate social norms. Even though this behaviour can be seen as positive for the endorsement of ethical practices through the punishment of unethical ones, it also suggests that situations can escalate to more emotional behaviours quicker with groups than with individuals.

Overall, research suggests that we learn from both the ethical and unethical behaviour of other people, and the presence of others we feel close to triggers social norms in good and bad (Gino and Galinsky, 2012). The presence of others can provide a form of social control on our behaviour, but social norms need to be made salient through ethics codes or training in order to prevent unethical behaviour from taking place when an opportunity arises. When norms are not enforced, behaviour decays, which shows that sanctions are important in maintaining norms (Andreoni, 1988). We imitate the behaviour of those we identify with, in-group members, when we are surrounded by people similar to us. When we are in the presence of others who are different to us, out-group members, we compensate for the unethical behaviour of in-group members by becoming more ethical ourselves. Moreover, rotten apples have a detrimental effect in organisations when the unethical behaviour is not questioned. This effect reverses if there are others from an out-group present in the situation, but such an outside presence is rare in workplace settings. Groups do however react more strongly than individuals to the unethical behaviour of others because the negative affect evoked by the unethical behaviour is stronger in group settings.

Key readings

Gino, F., Gu, J., and Zhong, C.-B. 2009b. Contagion or restitution? When bad apples can motivate ethical behaviour. *Journal of Experimental Social Psychology* 45, 1299–1302.

Three experiments show that people compensate for the selfish behaviour of in-group members when the behaviour is witnessed by out-group members. Compensation is triggered by a feeling of guilt. The study is interesting because it shows that being observed affects our response to witnessing unethical behaviour.

Keck, S. 2014. Group reactions to dishonesty. *Organizational Behavior and Human Decision Processes* 124, 1–10.

Two experiments demonstrate that groups are more likely than individuals to punish dishonest behaviour in others. This phenomenon is caused by a negative affect that increases as a result of discussions with other group members. The results show that relationships between groups are more likely to be negatively influenced by dishonest behaviour than relationships between individuals. Special care is therefore needed in such situations to maintain trust and a positive atmosphere.

Kroher, M., and Wolbring, T. 2015. Social control, social learning, and cheating: Evidence from lab and online experiments on dishonesty. *Social Science Research* 53, 311–324.

An experiment suggests that people are less likely to be dishonest when they are in the presence of another person. The effect of the social control however disappears when people learn about the dishonest behaviour of others.

Mock assessment questions

- How can ethical behaviours be encouraged through the enforcement of social norms?
- How do bad apples affect the ethical behaviour of others? Discuss both restitution and contamination.

Suggested class activity

Show the students the following interview of a Siemens manager about corruption at Siemens: https://www.youtube.com/watch?v=c5lYU_-W9SA. Ask students to summarise his opinion about his role at Siemens and what research findings might help to explain his reaction. Alternatively, show students recent headlines about plagiarism, which suggest that a high percentage of students may be getting help with their university work. Ask students how this makes them feel and how it makes them think about plagiarising themselves.

12 Physical environment changes behaviour

Learning outcomes

- Make recommendations about physical office features that enhance ethical behaviour.
- Specify and explain mechanisms through which the physical environment influences ethical behaviour.

The overarching trend in office design has been to change office layouts from single person offices to shared office space. The principal driver in such changes has often been a financial one, but architects and designers have also paid attention to physical office features that enhance collaboration and other desired behaviours. For example, Google has relatively large tables in its workplace restaurants in order to foster accidental conversations between people from different teams. One of the most recent developments in office design are shared co-working spaces that combine serviced offices with coffee shop culture. Such spaces typically have their own bars, events, and well-being classes. For example, Mortimer House in central London offers its users a Mad Men style lounge, fitness classes, and a meditation room. Research shows that the office environment has an impact on job performance and job satisfaction (Elsbach and Pratt, 2007). In the same way, the physical office environment can enhance or reduce ethical behaviours. Research in this area is still sparse, but there are some studies in which tangible features of the office environment have been examined for their ethical impact.

Zhong et al. (2010) investigated the relationship between lighting and dishonesty in a series of experiments. They expected darkness to enhance dishonest and self-interested behaviours because of the illusion of privacy provided by low levels of lighting. In one of the experiments, the participants were directed to either a well-lit room with 12 fluorescent lights or another less-well-lit room with only four similar lights.

Participants could see each other and the experimental materials in the dimly lit room, but lighting levels were clearly low and the participants were told that some of the lights were broken. In order to measure honesty, participants were given five minutes to carry out the matrix task where they were asked to find two numbers that added up to ten from a matrix that consisted of 12 sets of three digit numbers. The participants had an opportunity to cheat because they were asked to report the results on a separate sheet and return the matrix sheet and the report sheet separately without including any information from which they could be identified on the sheets. The results showed that the participants resolved on average seven matrices in both of the lighting conditions with no significant difference in performance (7.26 versus 6.95), but there were significant differences in the self-reported performance. The participants in the darker room overstated their performance by reporting that they had resolved on average 11.47 matrices, while participants in the better lit room reported that they had resolved on average only 7.78 matrices. Moreover, the percentage of participants who overstated their results was clearly higher in the darker room (60.5% versus 24.4%). The results therefore suggested that there is a relationship between levels of lighting and dishonesty with unethical behaviours being more prevalent in darker environments.

In a follow-up experiment, the same researchers investigated whether wearing sunglasses would have a similar effect as levels of lighting. They asked some of the experimental participants to wear a pair of sunglasses and others to wear a pair of clear glasses when performing a task. As with the previous experiment, the participants with sunglasses behaved in a more unethical way than the participants with clear glasses. The researchers also explored whether the unethical behaviour was caused by a sense of anonymity evoked by the wearing of sunglasses. The researchers used five statements to measure the anonymity felt by the participants during the experiment including 'I was watched during the study' and 'My choice went unnoticed during the study'. The answers were recorded on a seven-point Likert scale. Those wearing sunglasses reported a higher sense of anonymity than those wearing clear glasses (4.73 versus 4.01). The researchers also ran statistical tests to study whether the sense of anonymity explained the unethical behaviour and found that it mediated the effect of darkness on self-interested acts. As a result, the researchers concluded that darkness enhances unethical behaviours because of the false belief that one is protected from the scrutiny of others when wearing sunglasses. In an office environment, low levels of lighting can create a similar sense of privacy that fosters dishonest and self-interested behaviours, leading to a culture where moral transgressions are more frequent.

Researchers have also studied how the physical environment increases or reduces littering. In one experiment, the participants were found to throw leaflets on a floor of a mailroom when the floor was already covered with leaflets (Cialdini et al., 1990). In contrast, fewer leaflets were thrown on the floor when the floor was kept free of leaflets. The researchers argued that the physical environment alters littering behaviour through the activatisation of social norms. When the norm is a clean space, littering is reduced, and when the space is littered, littering increases. In a later study by the same researchers (Reno et al., 1993), they used a parking lot as a field study location and obtained similar findings. Interestingly, any activisation of the social norm through other people reduced littering from a neutral condition. For example, when an actor was asked to throw litter on the parking lot, littering by those who saw it was reduced in comparison to a control condition where the actor just walked through the area. Similar findings about space and behaviour have been established in other studies where mere photos of physical spaces elicited particular behaviours in alignment with social norms when participants had a goal to visit the place (Aarts and Dijksterhuis, 2003). In the experiments, showing photos of libraries and exclusive restaurants changed the behaviour of participants even before they were in the environment. The participants reduced their voice levels and enhanced their manners when shown photos of libraries and fine dining restaurants. As was discussed in the previous chapter about the effect of social norms, the environment can be a source of cues and reminders about social norms which have an effect on behaviour.

There is a scarcity of studies about the physical environment and its impact on ethical conduct, but environmental features have been included in a number of experiments as a manipulation measure. For example, in a study about time and ethical decision-making (Gino and Mogilner, 2014), mirrors were used to make participants reflect on their decisions in an experimental laboratory setting. When a mirror was placed in the cubicle in which the participants took part in an experiment, they cheated less than in a control condition without a mirror (Gino and Mogilner, 2014). In another study (Yap et al., 2013), the researchers studied the impact of space on ethical behaviour with the expectation that expansive postures facilitated by certain office and other space arrangements give people a sense of power which has been associated with moral transgressions. In their study, they found that drivers of cars that had ample seat space were more likely to double-park in violation of traffic regulations. They also found that limited desk space made experimental participants more honest than participants who had a larger desk area. The researchers showed that these results were facilitated by the expansive movements of the body that gave the study participants a feeling of power which led to unethical behaviour.

Existing studies suggest that physical spaces can activate ethical and unethical behaviours. For example, darkness reduces honesty and increases self-interested behaviours, while mirrors enhance ethical behaviours. The physical environment changes behaviours through a number of mechanisms depending on the space and the environmental features embedded in it. One of the main mechanisms may be associations between physical spaces and social norms, but more research needs to be carried out to understand whether this mechanism applies beyond studies about littering, using low voice in libraries, and using good manners in expensive restaurants. Other mechanisms relate to the sense of anonymity and self-reflection evoked by environmental features. A sense of anonymity makes people less ethical because they think this behaviour may go undetected or may not be connected to them. Self-reflection enhances ethical behaviours because people become mindful about their identity and moral compass.

Key readings

Cialdini, R. B., Reno, R. R., and Kallgren, C. A. 1990. A focus theory of normative conduct: Recycling the concept of norms to reduce littering in public spaces. *Journal of Personality and Social Psychology* 58, 1015–1026.

The researchers study littering in different physical environments showing how the physical environment provides cues and standards for behaviour. The article is particularly useful in explaining the activation of social norms.

Zhong, C-B., Bohns, V. K., and Gino, F. 2010. Good lamps are the best police: Darkness increases dishonesty and self-interested behaviour. *Psychological Science* 21(3), 311–314.

The researchers carry out several experiments about the effect of darkness on dishonesty and self-interested behaviour. The experiments show that darkness triggers a sense of anonymity that causes unethical behaviour. The article has become well known because of the study focusing on the detrimental effect of using sunglasses on ethics.

Mock assessment questions

- How would you expect privacy in the form of single-occupancy offices to influence ethical behaviour at work and why?
- What features would you include in the design of office space to remind people about the social norm of helping others?

- Physical features that makes us reflect on our behaviour are likely to make us more ethical. Identify such features and explain why you think they will enhance self-reflection and ethical behaviour.

Suggested class activity

Divide a class into two halves. Ask one half of the students to leave the room for five minutes and ask the other half to take the dictator game in a dimly lit class. In the dictator game, the students should indicate how many units out of ten units they will give away. The ten units can for example correspond to ten pounds. Students can be given the following information on a slide: 'You have been paired with someone else from the other room. Your task is to decide how much money from £10 you will give to the other person, if any. Your choice can be anywhere from £0 to £10. You will have one minute to make the decision. Do not talk to other students during the decision.' Students can report their decision through electronic voting. Once this is done, calculate the average amount given away by the students. Then ask the other half of the students to take the dictator game in a well-lit class, calculate the average, and compare the average from the two groups. Explain the set-up and associated research findings to the students and ask them for views about the difference in scores or, if there was no difference, why this did not happen in their case.

13 Detrimental effect of money

Learning outcomes

- Explain why exposure to money increases unethical behaviour.
- Design primes for wealth and money in experimental studies.

Cashless payments through cards and mobile phone applications are becoming increasingly common. In the UK, 72% of payments in 2018 were made through cashless means without visible money being exchanged (UK Finance, 2019). This move to electronic payments may be good news for ethical behaviour because research has shown that exposure to money makes people less ethical and helpful towards others. The philosopher Michael Sandel (2013) from Harvard University gives examples of the undesirable impact of money in his book *What Money Can't Buy*. One example is about a children's nursery that sought to reduce the number of parents who picked up their children late by introducing a monetary fine. The introduction of the fine however increased late pick-ups because the fine meant that parents stopped feeling guilty about being late and saw the situation as an exchange of money for a service. Sandel also questions the morality of allowing prisoners to purchase luxuries such as larger cells and fine dining while serving their sentence. Sandel is also critical about the ability of retailers such as Walmart to take life insurance policies for their employees meaning that they benefit from the death of their workers. In addition to these thought-provoking examples, experimental research shows that ethical behaviour changes in less extreme ways when people deal with money.

Experimental studies suggest that the presence of visible money leads to unethical behaviours. In one study (Gino and Pierce, 2009), researchers investigated the impact of money on dishonesty by creating two conditions, a poor condition and a wealthy condition, and gave the participants an opportunity to lie about their results in an anagram task carried out in one of these conditions. The poor condition was a room where the researchers had placed just enough cash on a table to pay the participants for the experiment. The wealthy condition had a table in the same place, but there was a large amount of cash, about $7000, on the table. In each condition, the participants were handed a stack of 24 one dollar bills from the table as they walked into the room. The participants were then instructed to create words from seven letters and to write them down on a work book. The more words they created, the higher the pay for the experiment. After completing the task, the participants were given 20 minutes to check the words they had created using a Scrabble dictionary. Once this had been done, the participants were asked to report the number of valid words on an answer sheet and pay themselves accordingly from the money they had been given at the beginning of the exercise and return the answer sheet and the rest of the money to a researcher located in the room. The participants had an incentive to overstate their performance because their payment depended on how well they performed on the task. Because they were asked to return the work book separately from the answer sheet, they were able to overstate their results without seemingly getting caught. The researchers had however marked each work book and were able to check whether the participants had reported their results correctly. The researchers measured dishonesty about the anagram task in several different ways with all the measures consistently showing that the participants in the wealthy condition overstated their results more than the participants in the poor condition. For example, 85.2% of the participants in the wealthy condition overstated their results in at least one of the rounds against 38.5% in the poor condition. Furthermore, the number of high level cheaters who overstated their results over several rounds was higher in the wealthy condition than in the poor condition (80% versus 26%). Just being exposed to a large amount of cash therefore made the participants lie to secure a higher payment for the experiment.

Other studies have shown that even sentences or images about money can make people less ethical. In one such study (Kouchaki et al., 2013), participants were randomly assigned to two conditions, the money condition and the control condition. Participants in the money condition were exposed to the thought of money through a word construction task where the participants formed sentences that referred to money (e.g. 'She spends money liberally'). In the money condition, 15 sentences referred to money and another 15 were neutral (e.g. 'She walked on grass'). In the control condition, all the sentences were neutral. Intention to engage in unethical behaviour was then studied through 13 scenarios. For example, one scenario read: 'You work as an office assistant for a department at a university. You're alone in the office making copies and realise you're out of copy paper at home. You therefore slip a block of paper into your backpack.' The participants were asked to record their likelihood of engaging in the behaviour described in each scenario on a seven-point scale from not at all likely to highly likely. The results showed that the participants in the money condition were more likely to engage in unethical behaviour (M=4.14) than those in the control condition (M=3.37). The researchers obtained similar results for other studies where they measured unethical behaviour in different ways including a hiring decision and a choice where lying led to a greater financial reward for the participant. In all these experiments, sentences about money altered the behaviour of the participants by making it less ethical. It is therefore the exposure to the idea of money rather than seeing real money that alters behaviour, but what causes this change in behaviour? What associations does money have that make people behave less ethically?

Researchers have suggested three primary mechanisms through which money influences ethical behaviour. First, Gino and Pierce (2009) argued that the presence of wealth evokes feelings of envy which lead to unethical behaviour. The envy is provoked by comparisons between a wealthy environment and one's own financial and material situation. Reminders about money may also influence behaviour through comparisons about the fairness or equity of situations. According to the equity theory (Adams, 1963), people evaluate fairness by comparing their situation to the situation experienced by referent others. Gino and Pierce propose that these comparisons go beyond people and include tangible cues such as visible wealth and verbal reminders about money. Behaving unethically in order to pursue personal gain under these circumstances restores equity and reduces distress caused by perceived inequity. This view is supported by the findings of Yang et al. (2013) who discovered that money, especially physically clean money, activates expectations about fairness. Kouchaki et al. (2013) provided an alternative explanation by arguing that reminders about money make people focus on maximising their own self-interest, even if this means that broader moral rules and other considerations are violated. Money therefore triggers a self-interested mindset that leads to a focus on personal gain where other factors become less pertinent and have less control on our behaviour. This interpretation is supported by the series of experiments run by Yang et al. (2013) who found that visibly clean money triggers a sense of fairness, while dirty money leads to self-interested behaviours.

However, when Gino and Pierce (2009) studied self-focus and greed as factors that underpin unethical behaviour in the presence of wealth, they found no support for either factor. The dynamic through which money affects ethical behaviour is therefore still unknown and may consist of a range of interrelated factors.

The experimental studies reviewed in this chapter have focused on unethical behaviour such as lying and dishonesty. There are also studies that have investigated the impact of money on helpfulness and other pro-social behaviours that are distinct from unethical behaviours. These studies suggest that reminders about money lead to reduced helpfulness and increased distance from others. For example, in a series of studies, Vohs et al. (2008) prompted participants about money in a range of different ways and measured the impact of these prompts on helping behaviours. Reminders about money reduced helping behaviours in all the experiments. For example, in one experiment, the participants who had been reminded about money donated less money to charity than participants in a neutral condition. In another experiment, participants were asked for help by another fake participant who was confused about experimental instructions. Participants who had not been exposed to money spent 120% more time helping the other participant than participants who had been primed with money. The researchers also found that participants who had been reminded about money preferred to work and spend time alone rather than with others. For example, participants who had been exposed to money were asked to indicate which leisure activities they would enjoy. The list of activities could be performed alone or with others. The participants exposed to money preferred solitary activities more than the participants from the neutral condition. Similarly, participants exposed to primes about money were three times more likely to prefer to work alone than participants from a neutral condition (84% versus 28%). The researchers concluded that reminders about money produce desirable performance-related behaviours including persistence on a task and taking on more work for oneself, but reduce helpfulness and closeness to others.

To sum up, organisations need to consider how the presence of wealth and other cues about money may trigger unwanted behaviours. Experimental studies suggest that only thinking about money without any physical contact can lead to unethical behaviour. Because of this, cashless payments may not be a solution for the negative impact of exposure to money on ethical behaviour. Studies demonstrate that unethical behaviour caused by money may be caused by envy, a sense of unfairness, or a more self-interested mindset. A sense of envy is caused by the realisation that one lacks resources that others have and this can lead to a feeling of unfairness. The more self-focused mindset evoked by money can lead to sub-optimal behaviour through the avoidance of others and team work, although money increases focus on the task.

Key readings

Gino, F., and Mogilner, C. 2014. Time, money, and morality. *Psychological Science* 25(2), 414–421.

The researchers explore the interaction between time and money and whether shifting people's focus from money to time increases ethical behaviour. The four studies provide examples of how time and money are prompted and measured in experimental designs.

Vohs, K. D., Mead, N. L., and Goode, M. R. 2008. Merely activating the concept of money changes personal and interpersonal behaviour. *Current Directions in Psychological Science* 17(3), 208–212.

The article provides a summary of multiple studies on the impact of money on ethical and self-interested behaviour with many useful examples of how to design experiments about the effect of money.

Mock assessment questions

- Why does exposure to money make people less ethical and more selfish? Identify three possible explanations and evaluate them critically.
- How can you remind people about money in experimental settings? Identify and evaluate at least two different ways.

Suggested class activity

Ask the students to find gender pay information from a company they would like to work for. They should be able to easily find this information because companies in the UK have been expected to report about gender pay since 2018. Ask the students to summarise the information for the company of their choice and let the others know how it makes them feel and think about working for this company.

14 More time, better ethics?

Learning outcomes

- Present and evaluate arguments about the relationship between time and ethical behaviour.
- Design experimental studies where time pressure is one of the variables studied.

Many everyday events can make people think that time pressure leads to unethical behaviour. Students have been found to engage in more a dubious kind of dishonesty when they have explained a late submission of coursework by the death of their grandmother even though the grandmother was alive and well (Ariely, 2012). If the students were confronted about their lying by a family member or a close friend, they would be likely to feel ashamed about it. In a more professional context, accountants allegedly accept weak client explanations and sign off work below professional standards when they are pressed for time (Svanberg and Ohman, 2013). Is the intuition and anecdotal evidence about the connection between time pressure and unethical behaviour correct? Do people become less ethical when they are pressed for time?

One of the earliest experiments about the impact of time pressure on ethical behaviour involved divinity students (Darley and Batson, 1973). The students were told they were expected to deliver a lecture about the Good Samaritan on the other side of the campus. They were divided into three experimental groups. A high hurry group was told they were already late for the lecture, a medium hurry group was told they should hurry to be on time for the lecture, and a low hurry group was told they still had plenty of time. In order to measure ethical behaviour, the researchers asked an actor to sit in a doorway the students would need to pass to get to the lecture room. The actor coughed twice and groaned when the students approached him. From 40 students, 40% stopped to help the man with 10% from the high hurry group,

45% from the medium hurry group, and 63% from the low hurry group. The experiment suggests that being under time pressure to accomplish a task can make people ignore opportunities to help someone in need. This behaviour happens even when people are prompted about ethical behaviour, in this case by way of preparing for the lecture about the Good Samaritan. The results are not surprising when considered in the context of studies that have shown that people become insensitive to others under time pressure (Moberg, 2000).

Similar results were established in an experiment carried out by Shaun Shalvi and his colleagues (2012). Participants in the experiment were asked to roll a die three times before reporting the result of the first die to the research team. The participants were able to roll the die without anyone else seeing the results. They were also told that their payment would depend on the outcome of the die roll: the higher the reported die roll, the higher the pay. The participants were asked to roll the die several times so that they would have a justification to lie. The multiple rolls gave them an opportunity to think that 'I accidentally reported the outcome of the second die roll'. In order to induce time pressure, the participants were randomly divided into two groups. In one group, the participants were given 20 seconds to report the result and in the other group, the participants could take as much time as they needed. The researchers found that the average die score reported by the participants in the high time pressure group was 4.56 against 3.87 in the low time pressure group with both of these averages being higher than uniform distribution across die results from 1 to 6. Participants in both groups therefore lied, but participants in the high time pressure group lied more. These results suggest that people on average behave unethically in order to pursue their self-interest and when under time pressure, they become even less ethical.

Shalvi and his colleagues conducted a second experiment to understand if the results stayed the same when participants were given a task without the two additional die rolls after the first die roll. The two other die rolls had provided a justification for lying and removing this source of justification could change the situation. In the new experiment, the researchers asked participants to roll the die only once and report the result of the roll. Like in the first experiment, they divided participants into two groups. In the time pressure group, the participants had now eight seconds to report the result and in the other group there was no time limit. The average for the reported die roll in the time pressure group was again higher than in the group with no time pressure (4.38 versus 3.42). This time, the average reported by the participants in the group with no time pressure was aligned with uniform distribution and these participants were therefore considered not to lie. The results showed again that time pressure increases unethical conduct. However, unlike in the first experiment, people in the group with no time pressure did not behave unethically. Shalvi and his colleagues argued that this was because they did not have a justification for lying readily available. However, it is also possible that they did not have time provided by the additional rolls to think about the consequences of behaving unethically. According to an old saying, the devil makes work for idle hands to do, meaning that more time people have in their hands, more likely they are to become unethical.

Other researchers have been surprised about the way in which Shalvi and his colleagues interpreted the results of their experiments. These researchers propose that honesty is the intuitive and automatic response when people are under time pressure because lying is cognitively more demanding and therefore requires time (Foerster et al., 2013). The researchers performed their own experiment to demonstrate the argument. In the experiment, the participants reported the result of a series of die rolls either immediately or after a short delay. The results showed that the participants lied only in the delayed condition, meaning that having time made them dishonest. However, when the researchers gave the participants even more time to report the die results, lying decreased suggesting that the influence of time pressure on ethical behaviour may not be linear. The immediate response is ethical, but becomes less unethical as time pressure eases and then returns to ethical when there is even more time.

What is then known on the basis of the existing experiments about the influence of time pressure on ethical behaviour? First, time pressure does seem to influence ethical behaviour with most of the studies suggesting that time pressure makes people less ethical. Where this relationship was found, the participants were either focused on another task like giving a lecture or they had an incentive to behave in a self-interested way to obtain financial rewards in the die experiments. These situations are similar to many real life scenarios where people are occupied by multiple tasks and considerations. In situations involving a primary task with the ethical behaviour being treated as a secondary priority, time pressure increases unethical behaviour because cognitive focus is on something else. In situations where self-interest is concerned, the impact of time pressure is less clear and more research is needed to understand how the impact varies over time and in different settings. Currently, there is evidence to suggest that the impact of time pressure may be U-formed with unethical behaviours increasing in situations with medium time pressure. Making a decision in these situations requires us to think through the consequences of being unethical to restrain the tendency to pursue our self-interest.

Key readings

Shalvi, S., Eidar, O., and Bereby-Meyer, Y. 2012. Honesty requires time (and lack of justifications). *Psychological Science* 23(10), 1264–1270.

The researchers propose that people become less ethical under time pressure because decision-making is instinctive and self-interested when there is little time to consider situations. They carry out two experiments which suggest that people need time and no easily accessible justification to resist dishonesty when there is a self-interest to behave in a dishonest way.

Forster, A., Pfister, R., Schmidts, C., Dignath, D., and Kunde, W. 2013. Honesty saves time (and justifications). *Frontiers in Psychology* 4, 1–2.

An experimental study is carried out to demonstrate that the experimental design used by Shalvi et al. (2012) may have been flawed. The researchers run their own study which suggests that the relationship between time pressure and ethical behaviour may not be linear.

Mock assessment questions

- What arguments can be presented to support the hypothesis that time pressure increases unethical behaviour? What are the limitations of these arguments?
- Give examples of the experimental designs that can be used to study the impact of time pressure on ethical behaviour.
- Studies have shown that lying is more cognitively demanding than being honest and from this follows that decisions under time pressure are more honest. Discuss whether this argument applies to other types of unethical and ethical behaviours, not only lying.

Suggested class activity

Ask two students to carry out an experiment where they roll a die three times and report the result of the first roll after completing the third roll. The die needs to be rolled inside a cup which is turned for the throw and the students can then view the dice result through a hole at the bottom of the cup. Give the students 20 seconds to do the exercise and let them know the winner of the highest die roll gets a prize. A timer can be used on a screen. When the students have completed the exercise, ask them the following questions: How did you feel when you saw the outcome of the die roll? How did the following die rolls change your thinking? Did you have time to think about lying about the outcome of the die result? If so, at what stage did you think about this? If you didn't lie, what prevented you from lying?

15 Summary

Behavioural ethics is an emerging field that has contributed new insights about the psychological mechanisms behind ethical behaviour and challenged some established wisdoms about ethics. Interest in behavioural ethics has increased in parallel to the development of technologies that have enabled researchers to study how ethical decision activate different areas of the brain. Behavioural ethics is often presented in contrast to philosophical theories of morality and ethics which seek to define concepts such as 'good' and provide normative guidance on how people should behave rather than how people actually behave. The focus of behavioural ethics is on explaining how people behave in real situations and what action can be taken to nudge behaviour towards a more ethical direction.

Research in behavioural ethics demonstrates that ethical behaviour is a product of individual and situational factors that come together in particular circumstances. Both individual characteristics and situational factors have the most significant effect on minor moral transgressions. When the ethical issues become more serious, the effect of these factors decreases. Nevertheless, ethical behaviour is malleable and can be influenced by triggers and prompts that activate individual characteristics and alter situational influences such as social norms. An individual's behaviour may therefore change in seemingly similar situations. For example, a sense of fairness can be evoked through statements about the importance of fairness with an impact on how an individual reacts to organisational malpractice (see Chapter 9).

Chapter summary

- *Gender*: no conclusive findings exists about the relationship between gender and ethics. Men have been generally found to be less ethical than women and men may also be more hypocritical about their behaviour. Gender differences seem to be stronger among younger populations before the differences narrow once people start working and complying with organisational norms and roles.

- *Values*: research suggests that the values of fairness and loyalty play an important role in whistleblowing decisions. A sense of fairness is associated with enhanced whistleblowing. The importance of loyalty explains by whistleblowing may lead to the ostracising of whistleblowers. Whistleblowing is seen as more ethical in individualistic countries and less ethical in collectivist countries where loyalty is an essential part of the culture.
- *Social class/wealth*: social class and unethical behaviour are connected in the sense that ethical transgressions are more likely for people from higher social classes. Attitudes to greed are one factor that underpin the relationship between social class and unethical behaviour. There may also be other factors that have not been yet discovered.
- *The moral equilibrium*: people engage in moral regulation to maintain a positive self-image. When they have behaved in virtuous ways, they can feel entitled to behave less ethically. This process is referred to as moral licensing. In contrast, when people seek to boost their self-concept, they engage in moral cleansing by behaving particularly ethically. Moral cleansing can be encouraged by reminding people about their moral standards.
- *Creativity*: creativity increases unethical behaviour. Based on existing research, there are two explanations for why creativity increases unethical behaviour. First, unethical behaviour increases because creativity enables people to find justifications for their self-interested behaviour. Second, unethical behaviour increases because the rarity of creativity makes people feel entitled to behave unethically in self-interested ways.
- *Social norms*: social norms may erode over time unless they are forced through positive examples, ethics training, and incentives. A mechanism of contagion and restitution takes place, meaning that 'bad apples' deteriorate the behaviour of others belonging to the same group unless the unethical behaviour is witnesses by members of an out-group in which case compensatory behaviour may take place to restore the reputation of the group.
- *Physical environment*: the physical environment has an effect on ethical behaviour through the activation of norms associated with certain spaces. Moreover, the physical environment can trigger a sense of anonymity which makes people less ethical. The physical

environment can also evoke a degree of self-reflection which increases ethical behaviour so that a positive self-concept is maintained.

- *Money and wealth*: the mere presence of wealth or other non-tangible cues about money are associated with unethical behaviour. This unethical behaviour prompted by cues about money is caused by the activation of a more self-interested mind-set, envy, and a sense of unfairness.
- *Time pressure*: the majority of studies have focused on situations where there is a choice between ethical and self-interested behaviour. In such situations, the research findings have been unclear about the impact of time pressure, which may not be linear. Other studies have investigated situations where ethical behaviour is a secondary task. In such cases, time pressure makes people focus on the main task with ethical behaviour decreasing because attention is on the primary task.

Bibliography

Aarts, H., and Dijksterhuis, A. 2003. The silence of the library: environment, situational norm, and social behavior. *Journal of Personality and Social Psychology* 84(1), 18–28.

Adams, J. S. (1965). Inequity in social exchange. In L. Berkowitz (Ed.), *Advances in experimental social psychology* (Vol. 2, pp. 267–299). Academic Press.

Amabile, T. 1983. *The social psychology of creativity.* Springer-Verlag.

Andreoni, J. 1988. Why free ride? Strategies and learning in public good experiments. *Journal of Public Economics* 37, 291–304.

Arendt, H. 1964. *Eichmann in Jerusalem: A report on the banality of evil.* Penguin.

Ariely, D. 2012. *The (honest) truth about dishonesty: How we lie to everyone – especially ourselves.* Harper.

Bandura, A. 1965. Influence of models' reinforcement contingencies on the acquisition of imitative responses. *Journal of Personality and Social Psychology* 1, 589–595.

Bauman, Z. 1993. *Postmodern ethics.* Blackwell.

Baumrind, D. 1964. Some thoughts on the ethics of research: After reading Milgram's 'Behavioural Study of Obedience'. *American Psychologist* 19(6), 421–423.

Bazerman, M. H., and Tenbrunsel. A. E. 2011. *Blind spots: Why we fail to do what's right and what to do about it.* Princeton University Press.

Blum, B. 2018. The lifespan of a lie. Available from www.gen.medium.com/the-lifespan-of-a-lie, accessed 31 December 2019.

Brambilla, M., Sacchi, S., Pagliaro, S., and Ellemers, N. 2013. Morality and intergroup relations: Threats to safety and group image predict the desire to interact with outgroup and ingroup members. *Journal of Experimental Social Psychology* 49, 811–821.

Brody, R. G., Coulter, J. M., and Mihalek, P. H. 1998. Whistle-blowing: A cross-cultural comparison of ethical perceptions of U.S. and Japanese accounting students. *American Business Review* 16, 14–21.

Carlsmith, J.M., and Gross, A. E. 1969. Some effects of guilt on compliance. *Personality and Social Psychology* 11, 232–239.

Cialdini, R. B., Reno, R. R., and Kallgren, C. A. 1990. A focus theory of normative conduct: Recycling the concept of norms to reduce littering in public spaces. *Journal of Personality and Social Psychology* 58, 1015–1026.

Craft, J. L. 2013. A review of the empirical ethical decision-making literature: 2004–2011. *Journal of Business Ethics* 117, 221–259.

Cushman, F., Young, L., and Hauser, M. 2011. The role of conscious reasoning and intuition in moral judgement. *Psychological Science* 17(2), 1082–1989.

Darley, J., and Batson, C. 1973. From Jerusalem to Jericho: A study of situational and dispositional variables in helping behaviour. *Journal of Personality and Social Psychology* 27, 100–108.

De Quervain, D., Fischbacher, U., Treyer, V., Schelthammer, M., Schnyder, U., Buck, A., and Fehr, E. 2004. The neural bias of altruistic punishment. *Science* 305, 1254–1258.

Elsbach, K. D., and Pratt, M. G. 2007. The physical environment in organizations. *The Academy of Management Annals* 1(1), 181–224.

Foerster, A., Pfister, R., Schmidts, C., Dignath, D., and Kunde, W. 2013. Honesty saves time (and justifications). *Frontiers in Psychology* 4, 1–2.

Frank, R. J. 1999. *Luxury fever: Why money fails to satisfy in an era of excess.* Free Press.

Franke, G. R., Crown, D. F., and Spake, D. F. 1997. Gender differences in ethical perceptions of business practices: a social role theory perspective. *Journal of Applied Psychology* 82(6), 920–934.

Friedman, W. J., Robinson, A. B., and Friedman, B. L. 1987. Sex differences in moral judgments? A test of Gilligan's theory. *Psychology of Women Quarterly* 11, 37–46.

Friesen, L.,andGangadharan, L.2012. Individual level evidence of dishonesty and the gender effect. *Economics Letters* 117, 624–626.

Gilligan, C. 1982. *In a different voice: Psychological theory and women's development.* Harvard University Press.

Gino, F., and Ariely, D. 2012. The dark side of creativity: Original thinkers can be more dishonest. *Journal of Personality and Social Psychology* 102(3), 445–459.

Gino, F., and Galinsky, A. D. 2012. Vicarious dishonesty: When psychological closeness creates distance from one's moral compass. *Organizational Behaviour and Human Decision Processes* 119, 15–26.

Gino, F., and Mogilner, C. 2014. Time, money, and morality. *Psychological Science* 25(2), 414–421.

Gino, F., and Pierce, L. 2009. The abundance effect: Unethical behavior in the presence of wealth. *Organizational Behavior and Human Decision Processes* 109, 142–155.

Gino, F., Ayal, S., and Ariely, D. 2009a. Contagion and differentiation in unethical behaviour: The effect of one bad apple on the barrel. *Psychological Science* 20(3), 393–398.

Gino, F., Gu, J., and Zhong, C.-B. 2009b. Contagion or restitution? When bad apples can motivate ethical behaviour. *Journal of Experimental Social Psychology* 45, 1299–1302.

Graham, J., Haidt, J., and Nosek, B.A. 2009. Liberals and conservatives rely on different sets of moral foundations. *Journal of Personality and Social Psychology* 96(5), 1029–1046.

Greenberg, J. 2002. Who stole the money, and when? Individual and situational determinants of employee theft. *Organizational Behavior and Human Decision Processes* 89(1), 985–1003.

Haidt, J. 2001. The emotional dog and its rational tail: A social-intuitionist approach to moral judgement. *Psychological Review* 108, 814–834.

Haidt, J. 2008. Morality. *Perspectives on Psychological Science* 3(1), 65–72.

Haidt, J. 2017. The new synthesis in moral psychology. *Science* 316, 998–1002.

Haslam, S. A., and Reicher, S. D. 2012. Contesting the 'nature' of conformity: What Milgram and Zimbardo's studies really show. *PLOS Biology* 10(11), e1001426.

Hessing, D. J., Elffers, H., and Weigel, R. H. 1988. Exploring the limits of self-reports and reasoned action: An investigation of the psychology of tax evasion behaviour. *Journal of Personality and Social Psychology* 54, 405–413.

Irlenbusch, B., and Villeval, M. C. 2015. Behavioral ethics: How psychology influenced economics and how economics might inform psychology. *Current Opinion in Psychology* 6, 87–92.

Jones, T. M. 1991. Ethical decision making by individuals in organization: An issue-contingent model. *Academy of Management Review* 16 (2), 366–395.

Keck, S. 2014. Group reactions to dishonesty. *Organizational Behavior and Human Decision Processes* 124, 1–10.

Kohlberg, L. 1984. *The psychology of moral development: The nature and validity of moral stages (Essays on Moral Development*, Volume 2). Harper & Row.

Koenigs, M., Young, L., Adolphs, R., et al., 2007. Damage to the prefrontal cortex increases utilitarian moral judgements. *Nature* 446(7138), 908–911.

Kouchaki, M., Smith-Crowe, K., Brief, A. P., and Sousa, C. 2013. Seeing green: Mere exposure to money triggers a business decision frame and unethical outcomes. *Organizational Behavior and Human Decision Processes* 121, 53–61.

Kray, L. J., and Haselhuhn, M. P. 2012. Male pragmatism in negotiators' ethical reasoning. *Journal of Experimental Social Psychology* 48, 1124–1131.

Kroher, M., and Wolbring, T. 2015. Social control, social learning, and cheating: Evidence from lab and online experiments on dishonesty. *Social Science Research* 53, 311–324.

Lehnert, K., Park, Y-H, and Singh, N. 2015. Research note and review of the empirical ethical decision-making literature: Boundary conditions and extensions. *Journal of Business Ethics* 129, 195–219.

Lifton, P. D. 1985. Individual differences in moral development: The relation of sex, gender, and personality to morality. *Journal of Personality* 53(2), 306–334.

Mazar, N., and Zhong, C.-B. 2010. Do green products make us better people? *Psychological Science* 21 (4), 494–498.

Mazar, N., Amir, O., and Ariely, D. 2008. The dishonesty of honest people: A theory of self-concept maintenance. *Journal of Marketing Research* 45(6), 633–644.

McCabe, A. C., Ingram, R., and Conway Dato-on, M. 2006. The business of ethics and gender. *Journal of Business Ethics* 64, 101–116.

Milgram, S., 1963. Behavioral study of obedience. *Journal of Abnormal and Social Psychology* 67, 371–378.

Milgram, S. 1965. Some conditions of obedience and disobedience to authority. *Human Relations* 18, 57–76.

Moberg, D. J. 2000. Time pressure and ethical decision-making: The case for moral readiness. *Business & Professional Ethics Journal* 19 (2): 41–67.

Piff, P. K., Stancato, D. M., Cote, S., Mendoza-Denton, R., and Keltner, D. 2012. Higher social class predicts increased unethical behavior. *PNAS* 109(11), 4086–4091.

Randall, D. M., and Gibson, A. M. 1990. Methodology in business ethics research: A review and critical assessment. *Journal of Business Ethics* 9, 457–471.

Reno, R. R., Cialdini, R. B., and Kallgren, C. A. 1993. The transsituational influence of social norms. *Journal of Personality and Social Psychology* 64(1), 104–112.

Rest, J. R. 1986. *Moral development: Advances in research and theory.* University of Minnesota Press.

Robin, D., and Babin, L. 1997. Making sense of the research on gender and ethics in business: A critical analysis and extension. *Business Ethics Quarterly* 7(4), 61–91.

Rosenbaum, S. M., Billinger, S., and Stieglitz, N. 2014. Let's be honest: A review of experimental evidence of honesty and truth-telling. *Journal of Economic Psychology* 45, 181–196.

Sachdeva, S., Iliev, R., and Medin, D. L. 2009. Sinning saints and saintly sinners: The paradox of moral self-regulation. *Psychological Science* 20(4), 523–528.

Sandel, M. 2013. *What money can't buy: The moral limits of markets.* Penguin.

Schubert, S., and Miller, T. C., 2008. At Siemens, bribery was just a line item. *The New York Times.* Available from https://www.nytimes.com/2008/12/21/business/worldbusiness/21siemens.html.

Shalvi, S., Eidar, O., and Bereby-Meyer, Y. 2012. Honesty requires time (and lack of justifications). *Psychological Science* 23(10), 1264–1270.

Svanberg, J., and Ohman, P. 2013. Auditor's time pressure: Does ethical culture support audit quality? *Managerial Auditing Journal* 28(7), 572–591.

Tajfel, H. 1982. *Social identity and intergroup relations.* Cambridge University Press.

Trevino, L. K. 1992. Experimental approaches to studying ethical-unethical behavior in organizations. *Business Ethics Quarterly* 2(2), 121–136.

UK Finance. 2019. UK payments market summary. Available from https://www.ukfinance.org.uk, accessed 27 May 2020.

van Prooijen, A.-M., and Ellemers, N. 2015. Does it pay to be moral? How indicators of morality and competence enhance organizational and work team attractiveness. *British Journal of Management* 26, 225–236.

Vincent, L. C., and Kouchaki, M. 2016. Creative, rare, entitled, and dishonest: How commonality of creativity in one's group decreases and individual's entitlement and dishonesty. *Academy of Management Journal* 59(4), 1451–1473.

Vohs, K. D., Mead, N. L., and Goode, M. R. 2008. Merely activating the concept of money changes personal and interpersonal behaviour. *Current Directions in Psychological Science* 17(3), 208–212.

Waytz, A., Dungan, J., and Young, L. 2013. The whistleblower's dilemma and the fairness-loyalty tradeoff. *Journal of Experimental Social Psychology* 49, 1027–1033.

Yang, Q., Wu, X., Zhou, X., Mead, N. L., Vohs, K. D., and Baumeister, R. F. 2013. Diverging effects of clean versus dirty money on attitudes, values, and interpersonal behaviour. *Interpersonal Relations and Group Processes* 104(3), 473–489.

Yap, A. J., Wazlawek, A. S., Lucas, B. J., Cuddy, A. J. C., and Carney, D. R. 2013. The ergonomics of dishonesty: The effect of incidental posture on stealing, cheating, and traffic violations. *Psychological Science* 24(11), 2281–2289.

Zhong, C-B., Hohns, V. K., and Gino, F. 2010. Good lamps are the best police: Darkness increases dishonesty and self-interested behaviour. *Psychological Science* 21(3), 311–314.

Zimbardo, P. G. 2007. *The Lucifer effect: Understanding how good people turn evil.* Random House.

Index